# Scrum Magic

## ULTIMATE TRAINING GUIDE
## TO THE AGILE FRAMEWORK

Purcell
consult
WWW.PURCELLCONSULT.COM

# Scrum Magic

## ULTIMATE TRAINING GUIDE
## TO THE AGILE FRAMEWORK

WWW.PURCELLCONSULT.COM

© DOUG PURCELL

This study guide is written from a combination of experience and high-level research. Even though we have done our best to ensure this book is accurate and up to date, there are no guarantees to the accuracy or completeness of the contents herein. If you discover any inaccuracies please email the author at **admin@purcellconsult.com**. "The Scrum Guide ™ The Definitive Guide to Scrum: The Rules of the Game" was used as the foundation for creating this book and was expanded upon—the authors of the document are the founders of Scrum: Jeff Sutherland and Ken Schwaber, who develop and maintain it. It is released under the creative commons attribution-share alike 4.0 international (CC BY-SA 4.0) and is free to access via the web at this URL: **http://www.scrumguides.org/scrum-guide.html**

Throughout this book several trademarks are used. Rather than being redundant and placing a trademark symbol ™ on every occurrence of the trademarked name, we state that we are using the name only in an editorial manner with no intention of infringing upon the trademark.

Corporate and bulk orders: If your company is interested in purchasing multiple copies of this book for employee training then send an inquiry online here: **www.purcellconsult.com/contact**

ISBN-13: 978-0-9973262-1-5

# About Purcell Consult

Purcell Consult is a boutique consultation firm that's obsessed with delivering sustainable results to their clients. The author of Scrum Magic is the founder of the company. He's a dedicated agilest and wants to push the envelope for Agile Software Development.

To subscribe to their newsletter and receive a free crash course to Scrum visit this URL here: **www.purcellconsult.com/newsletter**

To learn more about their coaching services, or to get in contact with the owner visit this URL here: **www.purcellconsult.com/coaching**

# Tips from the author

Thanks for deciding to invest in my book! To maximize your investment I'm going to provide some quick tips. First off, this book is mostly about Scrum with the exception of Chapter I, which covers other software project management strategies.

I assume that the reader has no prior experience with it and try to teach it as such. This book builds upon the concise 17-page Scrum Guide which is considered the authority source for the framework. The version of the Scrum Guide that was used for this book is the most up to date version at the time of publication, which was "English (July 2016) - Office Current Version."

In preparation for writing this book I tapped into my well of experience and also read countless academic articles related to software engineering, social psychology, and business management. I suggest for the reader to delve into these articles during their free time to expand their knowledge; the list of sources are included at the end of each chapter.

This book is segmented into five chapters and is orchestrated in a manner to help the reader learn Scrum in a sequential way. From chapters II through V there's accompanying questions to reinforce the concepts taught in the respective chapter. This is useful for those who want to test their knowledge or want additional preparatory materials to prepare for Scrum certifications. Also, "agile" is technically an adjective, and the specific term to describe the philosophy to building software is Agile Software Development. However, "Agile" is occasionally used throughout the book as a substitute for the term Agile Software Development. This was done to minimize the repetition of the three letter phase throughout the document.

Last but not least, the true key to Scrum mastership is to get your hands dirty by actively applying Scrum principles. Scrum is a versatile framework and it has many applications outside the software industry such as car manufacturing, human resources, pharmaceutical, and government projects.

# Table of Contents

# The Natural Elegance of Scrum

*Scrum* is a word that invokes excitement or disdain depending on the software developer you ask. A quick Google search will reveal many opinionated articles. Some will rave about the wonders of it while others will call for it to be brutally axed. Scrum is one of the most polarizing forces in the software development industry, and like many hot-topics there are fanatics and then there are skeptics. However, there's one thing that can't be denied which is that Scrum will stay in the software industry for quite some time as many companies both large and small have implemented it. What exactly is Scrum all about? Who developed it and what was their inspiration? Why is it so popular among software companies? Is it mere hyperbolic touted by those who have monetary interests in it, or are all the superlatives somewhat justified due to some undisputable track record of yielding positive results? In this essay I wish to unearth the answers to these questions. I also wish to explore seemingly unrelated connections between Scrum and team sports like basketball and even find connections between it to the natural world.

Scrum can be defined as a process improvement framework in which a structured team of cross-functional workers self-organize to incrementally and iteratively build complex products in cyclic intervals. The team relies on empirical process control in order to continuously optimize their workflow. The origins of Scrum can be linked to Hirotaka Takeuchi and Ikujiro Nonaka, who in January 1986 published their paper titled "The New New Product Development Game." It analyzed how companies like Fuji-Xerox, Canon, Toyota, and Honda were switching to a holistic approach to building products, and related this process to how rugby teams move the ball up and down the field as a cohesive unit. [1] This was a stark contrast compared to the then popular sequential methods for handling software development like the Waterfall Model. Under this paradigm teams would sequentially build the product meaning that a bottleneck in one phase could stall process. With the new method the team acts as a collective unit to build the product and since phases in the production process are overlapping it makes it easier for the team to adapt to unexpected events, like customer changing requirements or even market shifts. This new approach to developing products became the preference as the industry matured. Customers were demanding quicker releases of software which meant that a change in the management process was inevitable.

Jeff Sutherland and Ken Schwaber who are credited with being the founders of Scrum presented it at the OOPSLA conference in 1995. On Scrum Inc Blog, Jeff Sutherland stated that Scrum was modeled after Takeuchi and Nonaka's paper. [2] Six years after the conference marked a monumental time for software development as that's when the Agile Software Development movement was born. An important document in the software development industry was concocted from Feb 11-13 2001 known as the "Agile Manifesto." It was collaboratively produced by 17-seasoned software developers and highlights their philosophies of delivering quality software. There are many software development strategies which are classified under the umbrella term for Agile Software Development. Some of the popular frameworks include: Scrum, Kanban, Lean, and Extreme Programming (XP), while some of the popular Agile practices include: user-stories, pair-programming, continuous integration (CI), and test-driven development (TDD).

Agile is the most commonly used software development method by IT companies. According to a survey conducted by Version One, 95% of responders used some form of Agile and only 1% experienced failure—out of those respondents 72% claimed to use Scrum or some hybrid which makes it the most popular Agile framework by a landslide. [3] I decided to aggregate statistics to analyze the popularity of Scrum relative to another commonly used Scrum framework. I used three popular job searching sites which are: Indeed, Simply Hired, and Monster. Below is a table that displays the amount of results that were generated based on the queries "Scrum" and "Kanban." **Note. These numbers are likely to vary by the time you search.**

## SCRUM

| Indeed | 24,538 |
| --- | --- |
| Simply hired | 24,705 |
| Monster | 1000+ |

## KANBAN

| Indeed | 4,139 |
| --- | --- |
| Simply hired | 4002 |
| Monster | 1000+ |

Scrum popularity can't be attributed to simply seniority. The first book about Extreme Programming was published in 1999 by Kent Beck titled "Extreme Programming Explained: Embrace Change." The first book on Scrum was published two years later in 2001 by Ken Schawber and Mike Beedle, titled "Agile Software Development with Scrum." One can't argue that Scrum popularity is due only to its simplicity. Kanban is similar to Scrum minus the roles and "Sprints" so one could argue that it's *Scrum-lite*. So, what exactly is the enigma to Scrum's popularity? My assertion is that Scrum is king due to three primary factors: One, it's easily accessible to anyone that wants to learn the basics of it, two it has a track record of getting results, and three it strikes the middle-ground of being light enough to quickly learn, but with the right amount of structure for teams to eradicate some of the guesswork. When I ventured on my journey to learn Agile I found Scrum to be the most straight forward framework to learn. Anytime I discovered conflicting information I could refer back to the 17-page Scrum Guide™ for guidance. It was helpful to have a centralized resource that documents the appropriate methods but since the PDF was small there were naturally other questions I had about the framework that wasn't explicitly answered in the guide. There were various blogs and message boards that extended the topics of the Scrum Guide which was a nice complement. Also, Scrum has a track record of producing positive results for a variety of companies. Even though it was invented for the software industry it was derived from practices that were fostered in the manufacturing trade. This makes it far-reaching to some industries that one wouldn't expect. Below is a list of seven companies that have applied Scrum along with their results and source for further analysis.

| Company | Results | Source |
| --- | --- | --- |
| Adobe | Started in 2008 and increased product quality, balanced social life for employees, and better market responsiveness. | `http://blogs.adobe.com/agile/` `files/2012/08/Adobe-Premiere-Pro-` `Scrum-Adoption-How-an-agile-` `approach-enabled-success-in-a-` `hyper-competitive-landscape-.pdf` |
| BMC software | Individual team productivity increased 20-50% and employees felt more engaged and empowered. | `http://www.scaledagileframework.` `com/bmc-software` |

| Company | Results | Source |
|---------|---------|--------|
| Intel | Projects scheduled for 6 and 12 month durations have been delivered ahead of schedule. | http://dl.ifip.org/db/conf/ifip8-6/ifip8-6-2005/FitzgeraldH05.pdf |
| Xebia | Increased velocity with distributed teams. | Fully Distributed Scrum: The Secret Sauce for Hyperproductive Offshored Development Teams |
| H&R Block | Greater ROI, employee engagement, & employee morale. | https://www.braintrustgroup.com/case-studies/agile-case-study |
| Dutch Railways | Increased customer satisfaction. | https://www.infoq.com/articles/dutch-railway-scrum |
| Microsoft | Scrum+ 9 engineering practices improved quality. | http://collaboration.csc.ncsu.edu/laurie/Papers/ESEM11_SCRUM_Experience_CameraReady.pdf |

Out of these seven companies listed two of them are non-traditional software companies—H&R Block is a tax preparation company while Dutch Railways is a transportation one. Scrum is not only proven to get results for software companies but also for companies outside the industry. And, even though Scrum is light it provides a right amount of structure. It prescribes roles, events, artifacts, and rules which is a good start for companies that are adapting the framework. This is especially helpful for companies that were raised in a waterfall-centric culture and are unconfident on what to do during transition. Scrum is a journey and having access to resources will help companies set off in the right trajectory.

*Scrummage* is a term used in the sport of rugby to refer to the process of resetting play. It's important for the team to function cohesively in order to maximize their chances of winning. One of the famous quotes that iterate this concept is from author John C. Maxwell: "teamwork makes the dream work, but a vision becomes a nightmare when the leader has a big dream and a bad team."

In Scrum, the concept of self-organization and cross-functionality are paramount. Self-organization is a term that's derived from the physical sciences and denotes the ability for a disordered system to re-arrange its elements into an organized manner. It's been used to explain the phenomena in which players in team sports interact amongst each other showing co-adaptive behaviors without the need for any leader. [4] This cannot only be observed in sports but surprisingly in nature as well. One of my favorite examples is from the study of ants. These tiny insects have limited behavior but are capable of building walloping complex colonies that are efficiently organized. The ants interact with each other via a limited set of rules and without any top-down management. Not a single ant has ubiquitous knowledge of the entire nest, but instead works according to the stimuli of the local environment. The link between nature and process improvement may seem arbitrary at first, but perhaps there's something that businesses can learn from ants. After all, their behavior has been researched extensively and gave inspirations to the branch of artificial intelligence known as "swarm intelligence." Ants have been surviving since the *Cretaceous* period or roughly 92 million years ago, and have adapted to a wide range of changes. Change is something inevitable that Scrum Teams will face and they should take a lesson from ants and learn how to adapt to their changing environments.

Scrum is a buzzword that's in hot-demand. Many employers are looking for developers with this skill-set to become an asset to their teams. Scrum is proven to work as there are countless of case-studies verifying its prowess. However, even with all its accolades Scrum is no silver-bullet. In order for a team to increase their chances of success Scrum should not only be studied but diligently practiced. One can't learn to drive by solely reading books and watching videos. They must get behind the wheel of a car and correct poor driving habits through experience. In addition, one can obtain their license to drive but that doesn't necessary mean that they're an expert driver and should stop learning. There are many Scrum certification options available but even after obtaining a certification I would highly recommend to continue learning not only about Scrum but various Agile strategies. My motto is that you can never know too much.

# REFERENCES

1. Takeuchi, Hirotaka, and Ikujiro Nonaka. "The New New Product Development Game." *The Harvard Business Review* 3, no. 3 (1986): 205-06. doi:10.1016/0737-6782(86)90053-6.

2. Sutherland, Jeff. "Takeuchi and Nonaka: The Roots of Scrum-Scrum Inc." Scrum Inc (blog). 22 Oct. 2011. Web. 24 June 2016. `https://www.scruminc.com/takeuchi-and-nonaka-roots-of-scrum.`

3. "What Is Scrum Methodology & Scrum Project Management," Version One, 2016, accessed June 24, 2016, `https://www.versionone.com/agile-101/what-is-scrum.`

4. Passos, Pedro, Duarte Araújo, and Keith Davids. "Self-Organization Processes in Field-Invasion Team Sports." Sports Med Sports Medicine 43, no. 1 (2012): 1-7. doi:10.1007/s40279-012-0001-1.

# CHAPTER I:

# Software Project Management Mini Guides

Software project management methods like Agile have strong roots to the Software Development Lifecycle (SDLC). The SDLC is a systematic process to building software in increments—the software is analyzed, designed, developed, tested, deployed, and maintained.

The SDLC is the procedure that enterprise software companies use to build large complex software products. A company could decide to become a rebel and implement "Cowboy Coding" in which developers literally control everything including schedule—if a company does decide to go this route then all I have to say is good luck. However, most software companies have schedules that they need to meet and therefore structure is required.

One of the earliest types of the SDLC is the somewhat infamous Waterfall Model. Its popularity had dwindled over the years thanks to the rapid emergence of Agile frameworks like Scrum and Kanban. In this chapter you'll get a tour of three software project management methods: you'll discover shocking misconceptions about Waterfall, learn about the rise of Agile, and discover the non-software origins of Kanban. I would recommend studying different methods because it could not only make your resume more intriguing, but could also expand your management toolkit so that you can be equipped to fix any issue that springs-up.

# Waterfall

## BACKGROUND

Dr. Winston W. Royce is credited with discovering Waterfall—he first presented it in his 1970 paper "Managing the Development of Large Software Systems."[1]

The irony is that the version of Waterfall that had been given a bad name by software developers wasn't the version of Waterfall that Dr. Royce recommended for software development. Later in the paper he lists a more iterative model which he says is better fit for software development. It contains concepts that are familiar in Agile concepts such as involving the customer and a cyclic phase of: design, coding, and testing. Software is still a young industry, and in its infancy there was no standard for managing large complex products so the logical step was to borrow stable methodologies from other industries like construction. This presented its own set of problems because the two industries had many differences which caused the strategies for software development to evolve over the years.

## WHAT'S WATERFALL ALL ABOUT?

Waterfall is a sequential process to building software in which progress is viewed as flowing vertically downwards which gives a hint to its name. Since the process is sequential, every phase has to be completed before the next—there's no jumping order. In this model a strong emphasis on documentation is needed so that during each phase everyone involved will have an understanding of what's happening—this helps contribute to Waterfall being a heavy-weight software project management method. There are many variations to this model but a typical one includes the phases of requirements, design, implementation, verification, and maintenance.

An illustration of the process is listed below:

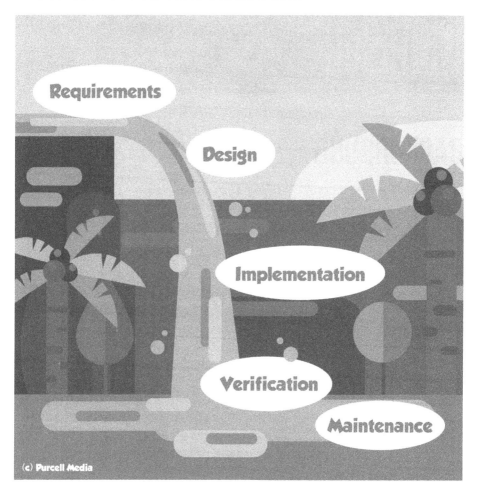

*Figure 1.1: Waterfall Diagram*

**REQUIREMENTS:** In this phase a meeting is held with the customer to gain a better understanding of what they want. This is critical because changes are highly disruptive in subsequent phases in this model. Therefore, the appropriate amount of time and dedication must be allocated in order to get a crystal-clear description of what's needed. Ambiguities must be removed at all costs.

**DESIGN:** This is the blueprint for the software product. Just like how an architect creates a technical drawing of a building before construction is done, developers should create a technical outline before they dive into coding.

Data structures, software architecture, and algorithms represented in the form of pseudo-code are analyzed to serve as beacon to the actual coding process. The modules are logically divided and software/hardware requirements are identified.

Flowcharts and diagrams are created to help developers visualize the steps and discover relationships amongst the system. This stage is crucial for the following one which is when implementation is done—without a design it's like trying to make a recipe with only a slight idea to the ingredients or instructions.

**IMPLEMENTATION:** In this stage the components from the design are translated into actual source-code. If the design is detailed and accurate, then it will pay dividends during the development process. The work is decomposed into small modules and coded in steps according to the design that the developers devised.

**VERIFICATION:** This is an alternative name for "testing." In this stage the system is debugged in order to discover defects in the software. The individual components along with the integrated one should be tested to ensure that the deliverables are error-free. Any defects in the product are corrected in this stage.

**MAINTENANCE:** This is the final stage in which all the system components are integrated and deployed to the client. The team should maintain the software in order to keep the customer satisfied. If an error is detected, an upgrade is needed, or additional features are requested then the team must go all the way back to the first step and traverse to the bottom.

# PROS OF WATERFALL

**HEAVY INVESTMENTS IN REQUIREMENTS:** The team will spend a substantial amount of time early on gathering requirements for the project. This could save the company considerable expenses as it's far more economical to make modifications to a project before the design and development have begun as oppose to afterwards.

**GREAT FOR PROJECTS WITH STABLE REQUIREMENTS:** If the company knows the precise amount of input needed in order to produce a certain output then Waterfall is an appropriate model. Since requirements are fixed in this type of project, fluctuating requirements is not an expected overhead.

**EASY TO UNDERSTAND AND IMPLEMENT:** Waterfall is in essence a simple five step model that builds sequentially. Any company can promptly learn and implement it to start building products.

**ATTRACTIVE FOR STRICT BUDGETS:** If a company has a strict budget then Waterfall may appeal to them. The company needs a laser-focused unwavering goal. Once they have compiled their detailed list of requirements they can hire qualified coders and then track their progress via milestones. Creating a software project with static requirements may be suitable for projects that are small in scope.

# CONS OF WATERFALL

**ALL REQUIREMENTS MUST BE KNOWN IN THE BEGINNING:** This may not be an issue for small projects, but for large complex ones this can pose a major issue. Software is an industry in which change is inevitable. Even if a company does know every detail they want for their product, unforeseeable changes in the marketplace could cause them to adapt while the project is in process. As indicated in figure 1.1 Waterfall is sequential and in order for a change to be made the team will have to collect the new requirements which is the very first phase of the model. This will cause the company to occur additional costs, time, and effort and could cause the project to stagnate or worst, never get completed.

**LINEAR PROGRESS:** The way that the model is setup means that each phase must be completed before the next one is started. An example of when this could become an issue is during the testing phase. Testing is done following implementation and if a stealth defect is cloaked during development then there's a possibility that it will become quite difficult to detect during testing. Defects in the software are much easier to fix early on—the longer a bug stays means the more difficult it becomes to identify and correct. This is known as *technical debt*.

**NOT A NATURAL FIT FOR SOFTWARE DEVELOPMENT:** I think it's fair to say that complex software applications are not coded and delivered as a polished piece without some bumps along the road. Software is developed iteratively and incrementally until the desired functionality is achieved. Since the software development process is dynamic in nature it makes sense to be managed this way as well.

**NO EARLY DEMOS FOR CUSTOMER:** The customer interacts with the team during the requirements gathering process and then delegates the development to the programmers. The customer doesn't get to see a demo until everything is done which is disadvantageous to both parties. The developers could misunderstand the requirements from the beginning and end up building something that the customer doesn't want.

**HIGHLY CONTINGENT ON STABILITY:** If a company is operating in a market that innovates at a slow pace then Waterfall may be a suitable model. However, software is no such industry as new releases are constantly rolled out. Change requests in any project disrupts the production rhythm, but the effects can be drastic for software companies using Waterfall.

# EXAMPLES OF WATERFALL

**MAKING A PEANUT BUTTER AND JELLY SANDWICH:** The traditional ingredients for a PB&J sandwich are as follows: two slices of bread, peanut butter, and jelly. The instructions are straightforward; you apply peanut butter to the insides of each bread slice, spread jelly, and then combine the insides of the slices together to form the sandwich. Applying the Waterfall model for a sequential process like this makes sense in this context.

**BUILDING A HOUSE:** If a homebuyer wants to create their dream house then using a model like Waterfall should be considered. It's important for the buyer to have a clear and stable vision of what they want for their house. If they want to make a change after the blueprint have been designed and construction is underway then it will be very resource extensive. The house will have to be essentially torn down, a new blueprint designed, and then the construction process repeated from scratch. Making small changes could be possible like door design, window style, and perhaps roof shape. However, don't quote me on that as I'm no architect.

# WATERFALL VS. SCRUM

To gain a better understanding of the differences between Waterfall and Scrum lets draw some observations. Waterfall is primary static while Scrum is flexible—change can be done in Waterfall but it's not simple, while change is embedded into the philosophy of Scrum. Waterfall delivers the complete product at the very end while Scrum concentrates on delivering small potential shippable units of product at the end of each Sprint. Waterfall doesn't explicitly define any team member roles or key performance indicators (KPIs) while Scrum does. Lastly, Waterfall doesn't specify team meetings while Scrum does. At the time of publication I compared the queries of waterfall vs. agile in *Indeed.com* to compare the results. Agile had roughly 9.65 times more jobs requesting Agile than Waterfall. This implies that while waterfall may not yet dead, it's definitely wounded. The American Group "TLC" signature song is "don't go chasing waterfalls" so maybe they're on to something.

# Agile

## BACKGROUND

Agile is a sizzling buzzword in the software industry and is the underlining philosophy that's adapted by many of the top software development methods today. Agile is commonly cited as being discovered on February 11-13, 2001 at The Lodge Snowbird Ski Resort in the Wasatch Mountains of Utah. A group of seventeen software professionals got together to socialize and have a good time. However, the mission of this trip wasn't just fun in the snow, but to also discover better ways to build quality software products on schedule—after all, it's not uncommon for software projects to be delivered late or over-budget.

Many of the attendees during this 2-day meeting had extensive experience in the software field. Some of those in attendance were: Mike Beedle who co-authored one of the earliest books about Scrum in 2001, Alistair Cockburn who created the "Crystal Clear," Ward Cunningham who developed the first wiki, Martin Fowler who's a pioneer in refactoring and prolific author, Jim Highsmith who created adaptive software development, best-selling author Andy Hunt, Ron Jeffries who was the first coach in XP, and both Ken Schwaber and Jeff Sutherland who are the creators of Scrum.

The wealth of software engineering experience at this ski-resort was as massive and intimidating as an avalanche. It was inevitable that something big for the software industry would be conceived during this meeting and the brainchild was the "Manifesto for Agile Software Development."

# WHAT'S AGILE ALL ABOUT?

Agile is a philosophy to developing software through the use of cross-functional and self-organizing teams. It's an umbrella term that encompasses several collections of light-weight frameworks, methodologies, and processes like Scrum, Kanban, and Extreme Programming (XP). Agile is considered suitable for software development due the unpredictability of the industry. It's considered the counterattack to the heavy-weight processes like Waterfall in which some critics believe is too regulated and micro-managed. The "Manifesto for Agile Software Development" outlines 4 values and 12 principles of the software development philosophy which was created and belongs to the original 17 authors of the Agile Manifesto in 2001. [2]

## 4 VALUES OF AGILE

1. Individuals and interactions > processes and tools.
2. Working software > comprehensive documentation.
3. Customer collaboration > contract negotiating.
4. Responding to change > following a plan.

It's a common assumption that items on the right are not important which is incorrect; it simply means that according to the philosophy that the items on the left should be given a higher prominence. In addition to the 4-values, Agile also has twelve principles which are listed below.

## 12 PRINCIPLES OF AGILE

1. The main priority is to deliver early and continuous quality software to the customer in order to meet their satisfaction.
2. Accept fluctuating requirements even late in the development process.
3. Frequently deliver software in short development cycles usually in the timeframe of a couple of weeks to months.
4. Business people and developers must collaborate daily throughout the project.
5. Motivate workers by giving them the environment, trust, and support they need to complete the job.

6. Face-to-face communication is the most effective way of transferring information among a co-located team.

7. Working software is the key method of tracking progress.

8. Agile is a marathon not a sprint. Everyone involved in the project should be able to sustain a steady working pace.

9. Special attention to technical intricacies and design is essential in order to strengthen agility.

10. Increase efficiency, remove waste or redundant workflow processes, and keep things simple.

11. Teams that are empowered to make technical decisions create the best requirements, designs, and architecture.

12. The team should delegate times at consistent intervals to self-reflect their workflow process and devise a plan to implement those changes.

# PROS OF AGILE

**FLEXIBILITY:** Also known as *agility is* the aptness of the team to adapt to fluctuating requirements during a live project. A project sponsor could request the addition of new features which can disrupt the plans for the development team, but a team that's versed in Agile should be equipped to handle these changes.

**QUICK INCREMENTS OF PRODUCT:** Compared to traditional software project management processes, Agile delivers small, quality, increments of product during a specified time-interval. This allows the development team to solicit feedback from the buyer and make adjustments on the fly when necessary.

**CUSTOMER INVOLVEMENT:** Agile allows customers to be involved in the product development process at an early stage and continually throughout the project. This keeps the customer informed about progress and will allow them to pinpoint changes that needs to be made ASAP which is more economical to correct than those discovered towards the end of development.

**EMPHASIS ON THE USER:** A common technique used for requirements gathering in many Agile based methods are user-stories. This is a snapshot of a feature from the end-user prospective which ensures that features implemented are beneficial to those who will use it.

**EMPHASIS ON COMMUNICATION:** In the *Agile Manifesto* people and interactions are given a higher prominence than processes and tools. Things like collocation, pair programming, and constant communication between developers and project sponsors is critical to correctly applying Agile.

# CONS OF AGILE

**ESTIMATIONS WOES:** It's difficult to accurately predict the completion of a project when a team has little experience in the domain, or when changes are constantly being made.

**DIFFICULT TO BUDGET:** Agile is a proponent of adapting to change—this can be negative if project stakeholders abuse this concept so contingencies should be implemented in order to keep the project within grasp of the sponsor's budget.

**FEATURE CREEP:** Since developers and customers are consistently communicating with each other this gives customers more chances to make additional requests. This feature creep could not only blow budgets and deadlines, but result in a heavy system with unnecessary features.

**DIFFICULT FOR RIGID PROJECTS:** Agile is suitable for projects with loose requirements. In order for developers and business people to gain a higher understanding of what's needed a development cycle should be executed to generate better insights, and changes adapted based off the new discoveries. This is a difficult transition to make for developers who have experience with the traditional approach that requires heavy upfront planning and more rigidity than flexibility.

**CUSTOMER COLLABORATION ISSUES:** Having a customer available during the development process is important in Agile due to rapid development cycles. However, maintaining a consistent line of communication with customers daily can be a challenge, especially if the customer is juggling multiple products simultaneously.

# EXAMPLE OF AGILE

The principles of Agile can be applied to a chef who's creating a new recipe. The chef may have a general idea of what they want to create like a pastry, but since they don't have a clear vision they'll need to experiment. After making something they'll probably have a better idea of what they don't want and will be able to gain a clearer vision of the end-product they desire—they may have to re-create the recipe several times before they get the right results. Adapting the philosophy of Agile makes sense in a project in which experimentation is needed. If the chef would try and apply a sequential process like Waterfall than they may find that they will be creating a finished product, and then starting over from scratch again to try something different. In Agile, since the creation cycles are short, small increments of product are created which makes it easier to re-create new variations. Remember, Agile is a prime candidate for projects with ill-defined requirements. New technologies that are not well known and will require heavy experimentation would benefit from the implementation of Agile.

# AGILE VS. SCRUM

I'm going to discuss the differences between Agile and Scrum in order to disambiguate the two to the reader. It's not uncommon for these terms to be used interchangeably in online articles and even though they're related they're still different. Agile is an umbrella term used to classify iterative and incremental software development processes, frameworks, and methodologies. Scrum is one of the many flavors of Agile and therefore has many attributes that's associated with it. In terms of binary trees Agile would be the root node while Scrum, Kanban, and XP will be the child nodes of it. Agile can be described as a general set of values and principles for building software which Scrum is an implementation of Agile with a set of specific rules and roles.

# Kanban Software Development (KSD)

## BACKGROUND

Kanban pronounced *Kahn-bahn* was developed by Japanese industrial engineer and businessman Taiichi Ohno and is an extension of Lean Manufacturing—It was implemented in Toyota to improve their inventory-control system. *Kanban* is Japanese for "signal card" and was used as a beacon during manufacturing to inform workers when supplies got low. Once this happened, a slip would be taken to a manager to replace the supplies—this was known as Just in Time manufacturing (JIT) and would reduce the amount of unused inventory. According to Toyota Motor Corporation [3]

Ohno's Kanban system was influenced by the American supermarkets circa early 1950s. When customers come to shop they would only select items that they needed when they needed (pull)—the supermarket would use a predictive model to estimate how many items to place on the shelf, and when new items were needed they would add more items to the shelves in the appropriate amounts (push). Ohno thought that aspects of the supermarket model could be implemented into the Toyota production line in order to eliminate waste and improve efficiency, and tweaked the model to work with the Toyota manufacturing process which gave birth to Kanban.

Workers would request (push) new supplies only when they noticed levels were getting low—the supplies were purchased (pull) in order to keep a steady continuous flow of the workflow. Kanban can be classified as a push-pull strategy and have been applied to various industries globally. Toyota has grown from a small company in Japan to the largest automaker in the world. There's no reason to doubt that their innovative manufacturing methods had a part of this which is why I decided to study them.

# WHAT'S KANBAN ALL ABOUT?

If you were to query "Kanban" into the search engine of your choice then you'll get some articles that talk about the manufacturing process, and others that discuss it in a software project management context—here's a way to demystify the confusion. There are two primary flavors of Kanban—one applies to the manufacturing system which was pioneered by Taiichi Ohno, while the other, "Kanban Software Development" is the translation of those manufacturing concepts into a software realm.

The distinction between the two is sometimes unclear because some authors use the terms interchangeably so for simplicity sakes I'll use the acronym KSD to indicate the software management framework. Some of the individuals who are considered pioneers in the KSD movement are Corey Ladas who compiled essays into a book back in 2009 called "Scrumban—Essays on Kanban Systems for Lean Software Development," and David J Anderson who in 2010 published this book "Kanban: Successful Evolutionary Change for Your Technology Business."

Kanban has been growing in popularity as an Agile based framework and my theory is due to its simplicity and flexibility. Kanban doesn't prescribe any roles or processes so it won't radically disrupt the ecosystem of a company. It's also extremely simple for a company to start implementing it to improve their workflow. A company can get started by visualizing workflow which s typically done by constructing a Kanban board, inserting items into the queue, and then partition the tasks by columns—a basic general setup is: To-Do, In Progress, and Done.

Below is an illustration of a Kanban board:

*Figure 1.2: Kanban board*

Sometimes the Kanban Board and Scrum board are confused with each other. The primary difference is that the Kanban Board should have a Work in Progress Limit. Here are the two types of boards juxtaposed with each other.

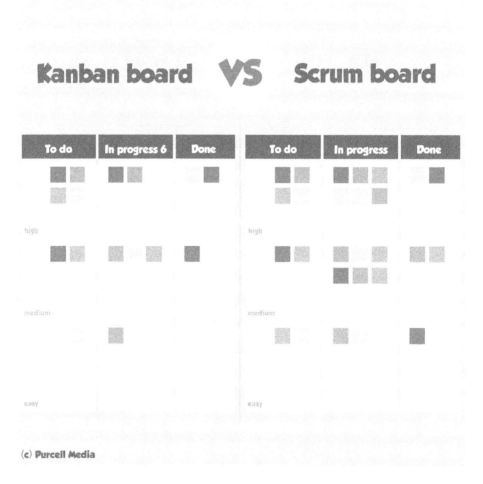

*Figure 1.3: Kanban board vs. Scrum board*

There are two main metrics in Kanban—Cycle and Lead Time. Cycle Time (CT) is the amount of time it takes the team to output a unit. A stable CT enables the team to gain a more realistic indicator of the workload they can handle, which aids them in providing more accurate estimates of turnaround times.

A stable Lead Time (LT) helps a team discover deviations in their production cycle. For example, if a company has a CT of 5 items per week, and one week they only produce two, then they know that a bottleneck occurred somewhere and the workflow needs to be inspected. The LT on the other hand tells how long a customer has to wait in order to get their product. For example, if a client requests the creation of custom software, then the time from when the customer places the order until they get the product is the LT—if it takes the customer 120 business days to receive the complete shipment of their software then that's their LT.

# PROS OF KANBAN

**CONTINUOUS DELIVERY:** This is a software engineering practice that allows software to be developed in short predictable cycles allowing it to be deployed at any point of time.

**ELIMINATE WASTE:** Software features are manufactured Just in Time (JIT) or only when they're needed.

**IDENTIFY BOTTLENECKS:** The concepts of Kanban can be applied to a variety of businesses to discover what's obfuscating the workflow. When output is slower than usual then that indicates there's a bottleneck of some sort stifling progress. The team must then identify the root cause and then resolve the issue in a timely manner.

**EASY TO INTEGRATE:** Kanban is light-weight making it simple for companies to implement with minimal disruption.

**REDUCE COSTS:** Since Kanban uses "pull" as opposed to "push," the company only purchases items when they're demanded for production. This strategy reduces inventory costs and minimizes the chances for unused inventory accumulating in storage.

# CONS OF KANBAN

**VERY SKINNY:** Since it's so light-weight it'll most likely need to combine with other Agile frameworks to deliver large complex software projects on time. A common hybrid is Kanban and Scrum which is known as Scrumban.

**ESTIMATION DIFFICULTIES:** Work continues until the items are completed so it can become difficult to accurately predict delivery timelines without additional measures to track progress.

**HYPER NON-PRESCRIPTIVE:** Since Kanban in its general sense is so simple to implement an unsuspecting company may think that changes will happen after they purchase a whiteboard, place post-its on it, and continue working the same way they did previously. However, changes to the workflow need to be made so implementing Kanban without any specific goals like removing *muda* (waste) will not net positive results.

# KANBAN VS. SCRUM

The similarities are as follows. They both are light-weight Agile based frameworks—their *leanness* makes it easy for companies to rapidly implement. They both in essence rely on a queue in order to store the outstanding work for the project—In Scrum it's called a backlog, and in Kanban it's referred to as a Kanban board. They're both empirical—you have to experiment with both in order to adjust and improve the process that the team decides to implement. Lastly, they both were derived from principles originally used in manufacturing. Scrum was influenced by the paper written by Hirotaka Takeuchi and Ikujiro Nonaka titled "The New New Product Development Game." The principles discovered in the paper were based on observations made from several companies such as Fuji-Xerox, Canon, Honda, NEC, Epson, Brother, 3M, Xerox, and Hewlett-Packard. [4]

Kanban Software Development on the other hand was influenced by the manufacturing principles innovated by Taiichi Ohno. The differences are as follows: Kanban is least prescriptive than Scrum as the latter prescribes roles, artifacts, and events. Also, Kanban lists an explicit limit to the amount of work that can be done during development known as the Work in Progress limit, while Scrum limits tasks by fixing the development cycle to a specified time-interval. Lastly, Kanban also uses continuous flow for development while Scrum implements fixed iterations.

# EXAMPLE OF KANBAN

I used elements of Kanban for the production of this book. Instead of going through a traditional publisher I decided to go the self-publishing route and utilized the **print-on-demand** method. In this strategy a book is only printed when a customer makes a purchase which eliminates the *muda* that I may have occurred if I were to purchase a crate of books.

# Chapter 1 Sources

1. Royce, Winston W. "Managing the Development of Large Software Systems." Accessed August 25, 2016. http://www.cs.umd.edu/class/spring2003/cmsc838p/Process/waterfall.pdf3.

2. Beck, Kent, Mike Beedle, Arie Van Bennekum, Alistair Cockburn, Ward Cunningham, Martin Fowler, James Grenning, Jim Highsmith, Andrew Hunt, Ron Jeffries, Jon Kern, Brian Marick, Robert C. Martin, Steve Mellor, Ken Schwaber, Jeff Sutherland, and Dave Thomas. Manifesto for Agile Software Development. 2001. Accessed August 25, 2016. http://agilemanifesto.org.

3. Ohno, Taiichi. ""If a Problem Is Left Unsolved and the Supervisor in Uninformed, Neither Kaizen nor Cost Reduction Can Be Applied. When There Is Trouble, Stopping the Machine Means Also Identifying the Problem. Once the Problem Is Clear, Kaizen Becomes Possible." February 2004. Accessed July 2016. http://www.toyota-global.com/company/toyota_traditions/quality/mar_apr_2004.html.

4. Takeuchi, Hirotaka, and Ikujiro Nonaka. "The New New Product Development Game." The Harvard Business Review 3, no. 3 (1986): 205-06. doi:10.1016/0737-6782(86)90053-6.

# Chapter 1 Rewind

In this chapter you learned about three software development methods which are Waterfall, Agile, and Kanban. Waterfall is a traditional heavyweight methodology in which software was built in the olden days. The current job marketplace indicates that its popularity had dwindled, and continues to spiral downwards. The modern philosophy for building complex software products is Agile, which is an all-compassing term for a variety of frameworks such as Scrum and Kanban Software Development—KSD, like Scrum is a light-weight Agile framework that has been growing in popularity. It borrows proven concepts from the Toyota Production System (TPS) and assimilates it into software propjet management. Software companies have been experimenting with combing Scrum and Kanban together to improve their workflow known as Scrumban. Scrum helps provide more structure to Kanban with roles, artifacts, and events which are missing in KSD. Accumulating a variety of software project management knowledge and experimenting with them is the key to knowing explicitly which methods is best suitable for the uniqueness of each team.

# CHAPTER II:

# The Eagle Eye View of Scrum

# SCRUM FRAMEWORK DIAGRAM

© PURCELL MEDIA

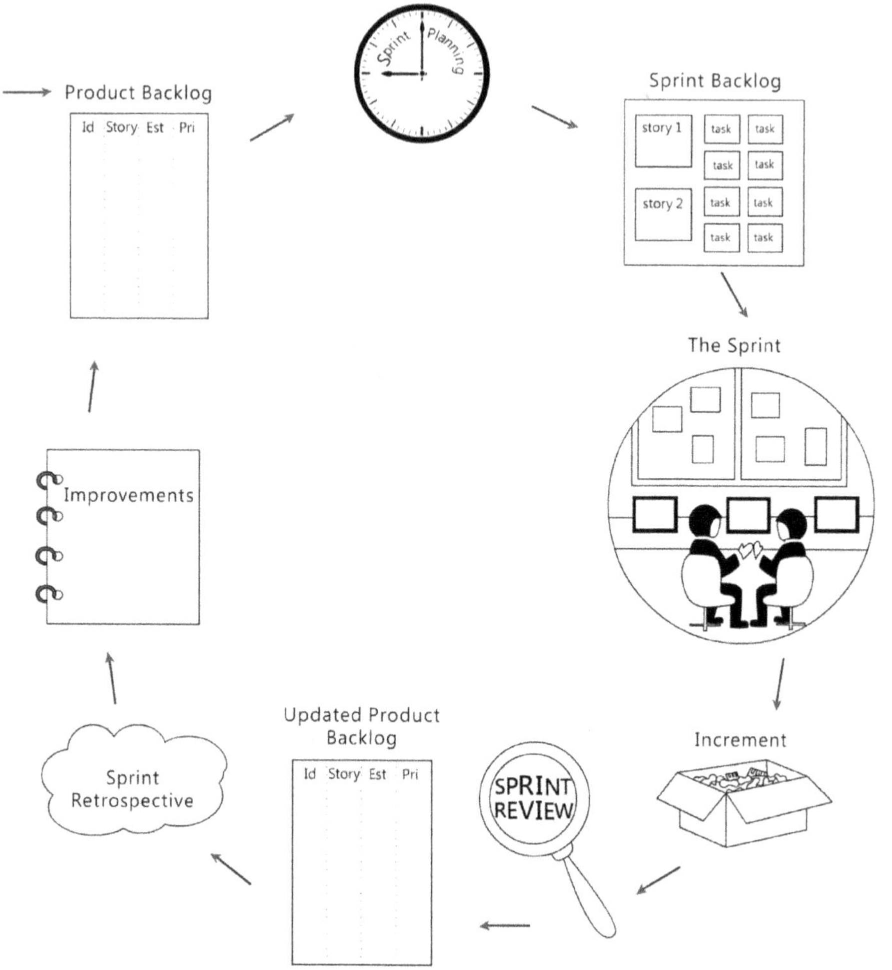
Product Backlog
Id Story Est Pri
Sprint Planning
Sprint Backlog
story 1
story 2
task
The Sprint
Increment
SPRINT REVIEW
Updated Product Backlog
Id Story Est Pri
Sprint Retrospective
Improvements

*Figure 2.1: Scrum Framework Diagram*

The goal of this chapter is to give you a wide-angle view of the Scrum framework. A gentle overview will bring beginners up to speed quickly by helping them understand the common components and jargon. I also believe that this approach is suitable due to the structure of Scrum. In this framework many components are interdependent.

For example, Scrum consists of roles, artifacts, events, and rules that combine them together—It'll be difficult to talk about an "artifact", aka the work the team produces, without talking about team member roles, rules, and events. The bulk of the chapter will concentrate on one of the most important components of the framework which is the "product backlog." A project cannot commence without the backlog—the team can be assembled, the rules can be mastered, but if no knowledge of the backlog is understood then the project will be stalled. For this reason I'll kick-start this book explaining the backlog and then expanding to the other portions of the framework. By the end of this chapter you should gain confidence in understanding the main concepts of Scrum.

# Product Backlog Mastery

Imagine that you have all the time, budget, and talent to create the product of your dreams. All the features that the product has will compose the **Product Backlog** (backlog)—this is the ultimate to-do list for the Scrum project. In the real world companies don't have unlimited time, budget, and talent—they don't even have this in the movies! Companies need to quickly bring their products to market while retaining quality in order to satisfy customers' demands. Learning how to create and maintain a quality backlog is a prerequisite to keeping the Scrum Team in-synch. A backlog should have a clear vision that's shared cohesively by the team so that they understand the valuable components of the product.

## WHAT THE SCRUM GUIDE SAYS ABOUT THE PRODUCT BACKLOG

Pages 13-14 The Scrum Guide™ describes the characteristics of the backlog under the heading Product Backlog. [1] I have combined them into bullet points below:
- It's the ordered list of features
- The first version documents only what's known
- It's non-static and ever-changing
- It's alive for the duration of the product
- It's the single source of requirements
- It needs to be refined

## IT'S THE ORDERED LIST OF FEATURES

It's essential that the items on the backlog are detangled so that the appropriate ordering is chosen. Scrum adapts the Agile principle that working software should be delivered early and continuously to the customer. [2]

In order for a team position to accomplish this themselves, they should first focus on developing the product features that deliver the most value to the customer. Rapidly building small increments of product helps trigger feedback from the customer which in turn helps the Scrum Team gain deeper insights into what the customer truly wants. To help illustrate this concept let's use an example. Imagine that someone reached a point in their career in which they're financially secure and want to build their dream house. Let's assume that they have done the prerequisites like purchase land, got proper permits, and have a blueprint for the house. When it's time to actually start constructing, the order in which the components are assembled is important. It would be odd to try and build the living spaces of the house without first establishing the foundation—therefore, the foundation would be higher on the "backlog" than the living spaces.

## THE FIRST VERSION DOCUMENT'S ONLY WHAT'S KNOWN

There's a high probability that the first version of the requirements will be extended with more details added later. The requirements gathering method used in classical software management practices would be to collect all the features about the software in the beginning. This consumes lots of time and would also result in monolithic tomes that would be difficult for developers to comprehend in a timely manner. Documenting every feature in the beginning stages is also risky because that's ironically when customers know the least about the product they want.

Older engineering practices like civil engineering for example have been in existence since Ancient Egypt circa 4000-2000 BC. Those early theories were used to help construct world wonders like the Great Pyramid of Giza which is still standing till this day, so the concepts for managing those types of projects have been battle-tested for millenniums. Software development on the other hand is a relatively new and very abstract field. It requires logic, creativity, and experimentation in order to obtain the optimal solution. Building software is complex and mutable, making it difficult for companies to know exactly what they need from the offset. They may have a general idea of what they want, but in actuality their visions would become more lucid as the product is continually worked on.

## IT'S NON-STATIC AND EVER-CHANGING

One of the principles of Agile is that changes in the requirements are welcomed in order to help the customer remain competitive [2].

In the Agile philosophy the team doesn't have to know all of the requirements upfront, they can learn on the fly and make the appropriate changes. Change in Scrum is viewed as a good thing—if the backlog remains static throughout the duration of the project then it's not being tended to properly. As the team collectively learns more about the product more items will be added, some may be removed, while others rearranged. This doesn't mean that a team shouldn't have a vision to work towards because they should—however, Scrum teams should have the mentality of change which is inevitable due to internal and external factors that are difficult to foresee.

## IT'S ALIVE FOR THE DURATION OF THE PRODUCT

As long as a product is on the market then there's an associated backlog for it. I like to refer to the backlog as the "soul for the product"—It'll remain until the product is terminated. Most products that have stood the test of time have evolved to handle customers' never ending wants and demands. Once a software product is *done* that's simply a façade as in reality it's just the beginning of a new journey. Once end-users test the product they'll provide valuable feedback such as bugs they encountered or other usability issues. The team will then process this feedback and go back to the drawing board.

## IT'S THE SINGLE SOURCE OF REQUIREMENTS

The backlog is the singular source for all of the requirements of the product. This means that strict application of Scrum prohibits the team from adding additional backlog—they are however allowed to add an additional backlog for each new product the company creates.

If the company has one big product then they may feel the need to have several different teams working on it simultaneously which is normal. Multiple teams can work from the same backlog which means that some type of convention will be needed to partition work and prevent overlap in development. The term for this is known as *Scrum-of-Scrum*. Since the backlog is the single source of requirements then all requests for the project should be synced into this one document.

# IT NEEDS TO BE REFINED

"Product backlog refinement" refers to the process in which items listed on the backlog are clarified with the addition of estimates, detail, and order. The backlog should be modified continuously in order to keep it manageable for the Development Team. The more detailed the backlog items are, the deeper understanding the Scrum Team will have of the tasks to be completed. Since backlog refinement is typically done towards the conclusion of the Sprint I elaborate on this concept more in Chapter IV. In the meantime just know that data is continually added to the backlog and therefore the refinement is an ongoing process.

# Artifacts, Events, and Values

Now that we have done a quick overview of the product backlog it's time to proceed with some of the other components of the framework. I'll provide a high-level overview of artifacts and events in this section, while more low-level elaborations will be added in subsequent sections. You'll also learn about the five values that Scrum requires for teams to adapt.

## ARTIFACTS

There are three artifacts in Scrum which are the Product Backlog, Sprint Backlog, and Increment. An **artifact** is used to denote work or value that the team produces. They are important to the team because it enables **transparency** meaning that everyone should be able to access it at any point in time to retrieve project updates.

## EVENTS

There are four formal events that are prescribed in Scrum which are Sprint Planning, Daily Scrum, Sprint Review, and Sprint Retrospective. The purpose of events is to minimize the need for extraneous ones and to maximize communication amongst the team. All of the events are **time-boxed** or allocated a maximum amount of time to occur. The reason for this is to optimize time and to not deviate from the agenda. Events are an excellent way for the team to communicate and to make send/retrieve feedback. It's encouraged for teams to constantly inspect and adapt their workflow to ensure that they're maximizing the process. Events are a prime time to elucidate transparency and inspect/adapt the process. All which compose the **three pillars of Scrum**.

# SCRUM VALUES

The **five values** of Scrum are commitment, courage, focus, openness, and respect. If only half the team is committed to obtaining a goal then there's an obvious disconnect amongst team members. The whole team has to be committed to success in order to strengthen their likelihood of delivering quality software on schedule. The Scrum Team must display courage and have the mentality of tackling extremely difficult problems as a unit. If all the team members are committed to helping each other for the greater good, then this will strengthen the courage of the individual team members. Let's borrow an example from nature. In the Yellowstone Park the gray wolves use strategy when attacking larger animals like Elk or even Buffalo. The numbers of the pack gives it courage in a difficult terrain. A poem by Rudyard Kipling describes it best, *"for the strength of the pack is the wolf, and the strength of the wolf is the pack."* Scrum Teams should aim to attack problems beyond their scope as a cohesive unit.

The Scrum Team must be focused on reaching one goal. The team should avoid trying to juggle too many different things simultaneously because humans are not naturally gifted with the ability to multi-task efficiently. The team can keep track their progress through a variety of methods like burn down charts which will be explained in Chapter IV. Openness is an important characteristic to get the team members to gel. An open channel of communication should be established in order to discuss things that's going well, things that needs improvements, and any impediments that are affecting progress. If something needs improvement then that won't happen with idle communication so a sense of openness is important to the company's culture. In order to foster a desirable working atmosphere employees should respect one another. Employees should be empowered, not bullied or treated as subordinates by one another or management.

# Internal Team Members

The Scrum Team consists of three key roles which are Product Owner (PO), Scrum Master (SM), and Developer (Dev Team). Scrum can be paralleled to the game of chess in that it has rules, roles, and a platform in which the game is executed, which for the Scrum Team will be the place they work. Every game has players and rules to specify the boundaries of play. In this section we're going to concentrate on the Scrum roles and their preset rules in the Game of Scrum. An unclear understanding of the roles can lead to poor implementation and thus unsatisfactory results.

## THE PRODUCT OWNER (PO)

The PO is the team member that's responsible for maximizing the value of the product and the work the development team performs. The Scrum Guide states that how this is done will vary across organizations but the common denominator is that they're responsible for managing the backlog. The guide actually lists five bullet points pertaining to the responsibilities of the PO, but I coupled them into three points since I found 3 of the 5 to be closely related.

- Ordering the backlog items to maximize the probability of reaching the business goal
- Optimizing the value of the work that the development team produces
- Making the backlog items clear and visible to everyone on the team

### ORDERING THE BACKLOG ITEMS

As mentioned earlier in this book it's important for the backlog items to be ordered so that the most important features are completed first. This line of thinking embodies the concept known as the *Pareto principle*: also known as the 80—20 rule, "the vital few and trivial many," or the principle of factor sparsity. This idea is attributed to the Italian thinker Vilfredo Pareto who formulated the concept in his 1896 paper published at the University of Lausanne titled "Cours d'économie politique." The paper observed the asymmetric economic distribution in Italy and concluded that roughly 80% of the land was owned by 20% of the populace. The principle has been applied to a myriad of fields such as economics, business, mathematics, and software engineering.

An interesting study published by the Institut für Informatik was conducted to see if the Pareto Distribution can be applied to the defects found in source code of 9 open-source project releases. The study concluded that a small number of files caused a large number of defects. If developers knew which files would cause the majority of defects then they can contribute more resources to writing tests for those at-risk files. [3] A similar concept could be applied when the PO is ordering their backlog—it's not appropriate to allocate maximum development efforts to features that end-users won't have much need for. Instead, prioritization is needed based on what provides the greatest value to the customer, which will be easier to determine once continual increments of product is released to the marketplace.

## OPTIMIZING THE VALUE OF THE WORK THE DEVELOPMENT TEAM PRODUCES

Agile Software Development, follows the philosophy that Scrum adapts has 4 values and 12 principles; two of those principles are relevant to this statement which is one, "business people and developers must work together daily throughout the project," and two, "simplicity—the art of maximizing the amount of work not done is essential." [2]

The first part stresses that business personnel and developers must constantly communicate in order to create a uniformed goal. If business people and developers have a different idea of the product then chaos is bound to happen. Things like late delivery, extended budgets, or a worst case scenario of incomplete projects could be on the horizon—therefore, in order to prevent waste from accumulating, the PO should be in constant contact with the developers to ensure that they're developing the right type of product.

The second point emphasizes the minimalistic approach to Scrum. The goal should be to build a minimal viable product (MVP) each cycle which is the smallest number of features needed in order to validate customers' response to a product. In Eric Ries book "The Lean Startup" he mentions how Zappos founder Nick Swinmurn created a MVP. He went to a couple of shoe stores, photographed the product to sell from his website, and then paid the owners full price for each unit sold. This MVP helped him validate the demand for an online marketplace that consumers can purchase shoes from. [4] The PO should verify that the team priorities are aligned through the backlog so that the customers' needs and wants are getting completed first.

## MAKING THE BACKLOG ITEMS CLEAR AND VISIBLE TO EVERYONE ON THE TEAM

Since the PO has complete jurisdiction over the backlog it's their responsibility to confirm that the items are clear to the entire team, especially the developers. The PO interprets the stakeholders' desires and wishes—since not all POs are technically inclined, they may not have a thorough understanding of the technical intricacies of a project. However, a deep understanding may not be needed if the PO discovers ways to compensate for this. Two common strategies are to collaborate with the developers or to delegate the tasks to them. Regardless of what strategy they utilize, the PO is the team member who's responsible for the backlog so collaborating with the developers on a continual basis is essential.

# THE SCRUM MASTER (SM)

The SM has a PhD understanding of the framework and confirms that the team understands and implements it appropriately. You can call them Scrum Coach, Scrum Sensei, Scrum Daddy, Scrumologist, or anything else as long as you recall that they're the guardian and protector of Scrum.

The SM can be classified as a servant-leader because they're a servant first and leader second—they serve team members and the entire organization. Below is a listing of services that the SM is expected to provide to the PO, Dev Team, and organization. The following snippets of information were taken from the Scrum Guide and enhanced.

## SM SERVICE TO THE PRODUCT OWNER

- Discovering techniques for effective backlog management
- Coaching the Scrum Team on creating concise backlog items
- Mastering empirical process control
- Confirming that the PO understands how to maximize value
- Understanding concepts of agility

## DISCOVERING TECHNIQUES FOR EFFECTIVE BACKLOG MANAGEMENT

Even though the PO is the team member that's responsible for managing the backlog, the entire team helps them to continually refine and improve it. The Dev Team may assist the PO with untangling technical dependencies or to inform them of any item that's out of order, while the SM could teach the PO how to arrange the items on the backlog in terms of stories, epics, or themes. It's important that the SM is continually researching and learning new concepts that can aid the PO in effectively managing the backlog.

## COACHING THE TEAM ON CREATING CONCISE BACKLOG ITEMS

Since the SM is the team member responsible for mastering Scrum they need to spread their wealth of knowledge to the rest of the team. One way to do this is to continually educate the Scrum Team on how to reduce the complexity of the backlog items. Remember, the backlog is the single source of requirements for the entire product, and if the product is large then more than likely the backlog will be as well. A large backlog can be difficult to maintain so the SM should coach the PO on reducing ambiguity in the content and refining the items to the smallest degree possible.

## MASTERING EMPIRICAL PROCESS CONTROL

A key component in successfully implementing Scrum is the concept of inspection and adaption. Scrum uses predictive methods like estimating the size of a user-story but that's validated via the empirical process control model. Having a method to track progress is critical for delivering timely products which the SM should assist the PO in learning.

## CONFIRMING THAT THE PO UNDERSTANDS HOW TO MAXIMIZE VALUE FROM THE BACKLOG

I like to refer to this concept as *checks-and-balances* because it helps regulate the decisions made within the Scrum Team. The PO shouldn't be making decisions about the backlog without any input from the Scrum Team. The SM should be to a PO how a coach is to a professional athlete. The player may be talented and experienced, but that doesn't mean that they're perfect, so the coach should recognize when mistakes happens and help correct it—the same concept applies to Scrum. The SM should non-intrusively confirm that the PO is correctly maximizing the value of the backlog. Doing so will ensure that the team is on the right trajectory to reaching their goals.

## UNDERSTANDING THE CONCEPTS OF AGILITY

According to the Merriam-Webster dictionary, *agility* can be defined as *the ability to move quickly and easily*. This concept is crucial to software development as it's a market that's constantly undergoing rapid advancements and innovation. In order for software companies to stay competitive they must possess the ability to quickly respond to change. A SM should be knowledgeable on how to keep the process agile, and they should share this with the PO. Some ways to doing this are making plans detailed enough to implement but loose enough to change, coaching the need for short development cycles, and encouraging the team to build the product in small increments rather than delivering all the product features at the end. The SM should obviously understand Scrum but it's helpful to understand the various frameworks and methodologies of Agile. Every company's situation is unique so it's inappropriate to try and apply a template of strategies to correct the issue. Instead, actual development combined with inspection and adaption is a general strategy to apply in order to optimize the workflow. Scrum may sometimes be appropriate on its own in one situation, while in others a hybrid of Agile frameworks and methods may be optimal.

# SM SERVICE TO THE DEV TEAM

Below is a list of services that the Scrum Master provides to the Dev Team which is taken from page 7 of The Scrum Guide.

- Coach them in self-organization and cross-functionality
- Assist them in creating high-value products
- Eliminate interferences
- Coach Dev Teams in non-traditional agile environments to make the transition
- Facilitate events

## COACH THEM IN SELF-ORGANIZATION AND CROSS-FUNCTIONALITY

One of the major differences between Scrum and traditional software project management strategies is that Scrum emphasizes empowering the Dev Team to make their own decisions. When a Dev Team is self-managing they're responsible for delegating tasks and deciding the way that work gets done. Management doesn't decide which developers do what, and they also don't micro-manage as the Dev Team collectively takes ownership of the code. When an organization grows large, granular management can become an overhead to the workflow. Instead of trying to manage the workflow of each developer the team should be empowered to manage themselves. This doesn't mean that there's no one responsible for tracking the progress because failure to do so would more than likely lead to late deliveries. Instead, management should interface with the PO to stay informed about project status.

The SM should coach the Dev Team to become cross-functional. Scrum works best with small teams as this decreases communication complexity, but small teams do have their drawbacks. One of them is that specialized skills may be a rarity making the removal of one developer a difficult obstacle to overcome on short notice. Therefore, a SM should be knowledgeable in the array of strategies in increasing cross-functionality and educating the Dev Team about it. A popular Agile method that elucidates cross-functionality is **pair-programming** or when two developers build software side-by-side. This method has been proven to enhance design quality, remove defects, and help developers acquire new skills. [5]

It's not a drawback for developers to have specialized skills, but it can become a disadvantage to the team if the developer doesn't share or acquire new knowledge. A master of some and 'jack of all trades' is something to keep in mind when trying to condition the Dev Team to become cross-functional. They shouldn't be siloed into separate roles, but instead continually collaborate with other developers to augment their skills.

## ASSIST THEM IN CREATING HIGH-VALUE PRODUCTS

Even though the Dev Team is in charge with building the product the SM can still have an impact on the end-result. For example, if the Dev Team is producing buggy software then a unit-testing plan can be suggested by the SM—if the Dev Team is having issues delivering timely software then the SM can suggest for the Dev Team to take a more proactive approach in monitoring the daily work remaining—if the Dev Team is having technical difficulties due to limited skills then the SM can suggest pair-programming. The SM should be keeping an eye on the Dev Team and recognize when assistance is needed in order to help them output and build solid products.

## ELIMINATE INTERFERENCES

A common misconception about the SM's responsibility is what they do on a day-by-day basis. One of their main priorities is they remove impediments from the Dev Team which could be an exhaustive task in itself. I prefer to classify impediments as internal or external. An example of an internal impediment is one that deals with lack of knowledge about the Scrum process, while an external one could be managers demanding that developers use certain types of tools without their input. The SM must manage both types of impediments in order to keep the Dev Team's workflow continuous. Since the Scrum Guide doesn't suggest any specific procedures here's some suggestions: One, categorize impediments with the goal of extrapolating information from them. The SM may notice that the impediments share a common theme of stakeholder intervention so they could consider hosting a workshop to educate them about the benefits of self-organization and cross-functionality. Two, once impediments are discovered it's critical that the SM makes it visible to the Dev Team so that they can assist with finding a solution. If the removal of the impediment is critical then it could be added as a backlog item with the consensus of the PO. Third, the SM should develop an efficient means of managing the dissolution of the impediments. Too many impediments could indicate that they're not being resolved in a timely manner. Having a congestion of impediments could disrupt the development rhythm and jeopardize the delivery date of software. Identifying impediments is a start and making them transparent is helpful, but those steps are meaningless if impediments linger within the workflow. Some impediments are more threatening than others so the SM should develop an appropriate mechanism to prioritize their removal.

## COACH DEV TEAM'S IN NON-TRADITIONAL AGILE ENVIRONMENTS MAKE THE TRANSITION

The Scrum Master is a role that requires multiple hats. Depending on the situation they may need to put on their facilitating, teaching, or coaching hat. By default the SM is the team's coach in Scrum, but what exactly does coaching entails? According to the Merriam-Webster Dictionary, a coach is *someone that teaches and trains the members of a sports team along with making decisions about how they play*. Coaching derived its roots from the education field and saw a surge of growth in the mid-90s. There are now several organizations dedicated to creating standards for coaching such as the International Coach Federation, International Association for Coaching, and European Coaching and Mentoring Council. I have synthesized several studies to discover patterns that are associated with quality coaching. An article published by the Harvard Business Review gave an interesting overview on this subject. According to the study, 140 leading coaches were surveyed, and five experts commented on the data. The study reported that 48% of the coaches surveyed were brought in to develop high potential employees or facilitate transition. [6]

This indicates that organizations value key employees and will continually invest money into strengthening their skill-sets—it also reveals that organizations are looking for ways to innovate as transitioning requires disrupting the current culture of the company. The study also listed key characteristics that companies should look for when hiring a coach such as: experience of coaching in a similar setting, clear methodology, quality of client list, ability to measure ROI, and certification in a proven coaching method. [6]

Another article published on the Harvard Business Review states that in order for a manager to be effective they must possess coaching abilities. [7]

This further emphasizes the value that quality coaching practices can have on teams. A paper specific to Agile Software Development confirmed the theory that rewards and punishments used in classical management is good in the short term for controlling human behavior but is not sustainable. A counter to that type of management style is coaching—common patterns that emerged from successful coaching were analyzed such as: mutual trustful relationship, structured communication, and change through the use of experimental learning. [8]

A Scrum Master should actively seek out ways to become a better coach. Building relationships with the Dev Team and encouraging them to become the best they can be could pay off dividends for the company.

## FACILITATING EVENTS

The Scrum Master is in charge with orchestrating the prescribed events in the Scrum framework. The Scrum Guide provides recommended events along with checkpoints for when to host them. However, there may also be occasions in which the Scrum Master may be required to administer events impromptu. Events in Scrum are important opportunities for inspection and adaption. The Scrum Master acts as the referee for the events and makes sure that the team players are correctly applying the rules to the game. They ensure that the events are held, the rules are followed, and that the attendees understand its purpose. Without their governance it's a possibility that the Scrum Team may deviate from its purpose. Therefore, it's critical that the Scrum Master has a strong expertise of the events so that they can transfer this knowledge to the rest of the Scrum Team.

## SM SERVICE TO THE ORGANIZATION

The Scrum Master serves not only the Scrum Team but also those outside of it who are part of the organization. The Scrum Master role therefore has the largest range compared to any other team member. The Scrum Guide lists five points that describe the Scrum Master's service to the organization. Out of those five I found two that overlapped and therefore condensed it. Below is a list of services that the SM provides the organization:

- Leading the organization in Scrum adaption
- Helping employees and stakeholders understand Scrum and the empirical process
- Planning Scrum implementations in the organization
- Working with other Scrum Masters to improve the effectiveness of Scrum within the organization

## LEADING THE ORGANIZATION IN SCRUM ADAPTION

Getting one person to change a habit is difficult, getting an entire organization to do so requires magic. A Scrum Master must be equipped with the skills to assist the organization with adapting the principles of Scrum. This is not an easy task; especially if the organization has a history of using traditional software project management methods which are more manager-centric. The SM must be ok with disrupting the workplace if it will produce a better company in the long run. It's important for the Scrum Master to have strong leadership skills coupled with a deep understanding of the new system that will be integrated into the organization. There are many types of leadership styles, but the one I would recommend studying for this type of context is transformational leadership. Under this style the leader's main purpose is to indoctrinate a new line of thinking in the employees. In order for change to be complete, the employees must be indoctrinated; otherwise what progress was made will only be temporary. Employees will be more receptive to change if the alternative is more attractive than the status quo. A transformational leader must align employees' desires with that of the company. It's not irrational for employees to have their own self-interest, but a transformational leader must get employees to think beyond that for the good of the company. Typical characteristics of transformational leader possess are charisma, the ability to inspire, and the capacity to arouse intellectual stimulation. [9]

## HELP EMPLOYEES AND STAKEHOLDERS UNDERSTAND SCRUM AND THE EMPIRICAL PROCESS CONTROL

The employees outside of a typical Scrum Team could include: customer service, sales account manager, market research analyst, and marketing executive. Believe it or not, all of them could benefit by applying Scrum to their workflow. Let's assume that after five months company XYZ have developed a consistent cadence and can quickly roll out new features of their product. It's a good idea for the sales department to understand Scrum so that they can add it as a selling point to prospective clients. Another example is that it's a good idea for the marketing department to understand Scrum since it has been successfully implemented in this field. They can use it to improve their marketing process and discover new ways to generate more traffic, leads, engagement, etc. Marketing relies a lot on experimental learning, and using past campaigns to improve future ones is a common strategy. Having the Scrum Team become as efficient as possible is great, but having all of the employees of a company optimize their performance is not a bad idea either.

## PLANNING SCRUM IMPLEMENTATIONS IN THE ORGANIZATION

If the individuals that are expected to apply Scrum don't fully understand it then progress won't be made. Therefore, the Scrum Master should become an effective educator. Many companies are investing in Scrum training as a result of this. In order to be effective, the Scrum Master should study the principles of teaching. There are many different strategies to doing this—my motto is the best strategy is the one the team prefers. You can always use polling methods to understand what type of strategy they prefer, or you can try a method, analyze, and try something different if results are unsatisfactory. Some common methods for instruction are: lecturing, demonstration, and collaboration. Lectures are one of the most popular examples of teaching, especially in universities in which lecture halls can fill a surplus of a hundred students. This method is ideal as it can spread the information to a large audience in an efficient manner. The drawback to this method is that it's passive learning and studies have indicated that interactive learning yields better results [10].

Teaching by demonstration is an example of interactive teaching and involves explaining something through the use of examples or experiments. This is a common strategy that's used by science instructors to help students form connections between theories. For example a chemistry instructor may utilize iodine clock reaction to display chemical kinetics in action. Collaboration is another effective strategy for teaching as it allows the students to actively participate in the learning process. One common strategy for inducing collaboration amongst a team is discussions. There are many different formats to doing this such as Fishbowl, Unconference, and Knowledge Café.

Various formats should be experimented with in order to determine which one is most beneficial to the team. In addition to teaching, some form of assessment needs to be incorporated in order to measure the progress of students. Some common strategies for assessments are group projects, student portfolios, and quizzes/tests.

## WORK WITH OTHER SCRUM MASTERS TO IMPROVE SCRUM IN THE ORGANIZATION

Just because someone is a Scrum Master doesn't mean that they have all of the answers regarding the Scrum universe. Just like teachers have to undergo continuous professional development to keep their skills relevant, so should Scrum Masters. Teachers in a school may talk with their peers about teaching strategies that worked best for them, and Scrum Masters should do the same. This discussion can lead to better understanding of the organization along with the best strategies on how to make those changes stick. In addition, it can help Scrum Masters gain new insights to problems that their team is facing.

# THE DEVELOPMENT (DEV) TEAM

The Dev Team is the team members who are responsible for building the actual product. The potentially shippable code that the Dev Team produces at the end of a development cycle is known as an "Increment." The Dev Team is supposed to be empowered so that they can figure out how they get work done. Below are a collection of bullets that describes the responsibilities of the Dev Team taken from page 6 of The Scrum Guide.

- They're self-organizing
- They're cross-functional
- They're no titles other than Developer
- They're no sub-teams
- Accountability belongs to the Dev Team as a whole

## THEY'RE SELF-ORGANIZING

An Agile principle that's relevant to self-organization is as follows: "build projects around motivated individuals, give them the environment they need, and trust them to get the job done."[2] This philosophy is in direct alignment of **self-organization** which is the process in which teams are empowered to make their own decisions without the influence of management. In layman terms, since technical workers have a higher understanding of this domain than non-technical managers, it's not a bad idea to allow them the rights to make technical decisions such as what design to use, or the best way of going about building the system architecture. A case-study about the patterns of self-organized teams discovered that autonomy combined with communication and collaboration are critical components for building self-organizing teams. [11]

## THEY'RE CROSS-FUNCTIONAL

Since Scrum teams are small it's important that the developers are cross-functional. This is the act in which developers acquire the skill-sets of each team member. The Dev Team should collaborate and create a method for transferring knowledge amongst each other. One of the benefits to making a Scrum Team cross-functional is that there is a higher chance in product success. [12]

If a developer of a Scrum Team leaves during the middle of development then this could be a major obstacle for the team to recover from in a short amount of time. However, if the team is cross-functional then they can absorb the loss better and can self-organize the outstanding work.

## THEY'RE NO TITLES OTHER THAN DEVELOPER

Scrum doesn't explicitly define any titles for seniority on the Dev Team. The paper "job titles across organizations" discovered that job titles proliferated most in organizations that are large, bureaucratic rely on firm-specific skills, have a professional workplace, and are in institutional sectors. [13]

Perhaps this is one of the reasons that The Scrum Guide prohibits any titles for members of the Dev Team. Another theory is that by excluding titles the team will have an easier time of implementing self-organization and cross-functionality. This mentality can be useful for bringing lesser experienced programmers up to speed quickly. For example, a rookie developer could pair-program with a more experienced one. In addition, the exclusion of titles decreases specialization and promotes collective ownership in the code. For example, since there's no specific role for testers in Scrum the entire Dev Team must do testing. Not attributing any specific titles to the Dev Team is not a popular topic amongst some developers. It's not unreasonable to assume that employees would like to advance in their career, and by not assigning a specific title to a developer such as junior vs. senior developer it's difficult for this to happen.

## THEY'RE NO SUB-TEAMS

The only individuals that make it to the Dev Team are the developers. The Dev Team are the ones that design, code, test, and integrate the product. Since each member is expected to contribute to this, there's in theory no need for a specific tester role in the Scrum Team. In addition, other roles that may be found in other project management methods like business analysts are not recognized as being part of the Dev Team. It's possible however for them to be included outside of the Scrum Team, perhaps as a stakeholder.

## ACCOUNTABILITY BELONGS TO THE DEV TEAM AS A WHOLE

As previously mentioned, each developer plays a role in the designing, coding, testing, and integrating of the software. Even though some developers may come to the team with specialized skill-sets they're still expected to acquire additional ones, become cross-functional, and share in the accountability for the entire code. The developers shouldn't be solely concerned with the work they're doing, but should also be concerned about the entire code base.

# Stakeholders

Even though stakeholders are not officially declared in the Scrum Guide as being part of the team, they're still important for the success of the product. There's some ambiguity about the term stakeholder— it's used several times in the Study Guide but it's not explicitly defined. A stakeholder is a person, group, or organization that may be affected by the outcome of a project, program, or portfolio. Even though the term is typically used to refer to management or customers, the Product Owner is sometimes referred to as a stakeholder as they represent them to the Scrum Team. More examples of stakeholders include end-users, investors, project sponsors, support, portfolio manager, domain experts, and salespeople.

# Team Size

Now that we have discussed the roles behind a Scrum Team it's time to discuss some other important attributes, such as the size. To kick-start this topic I'm going to provide a quote from the Scrum Guide: "fewer than three Development Team members decrease interaction and results in smaller productivity gains. Having more than nine members requires too much coordination." [14]

Therefore, since a Scrum team consists of 1 PO, 1 SM, and 3-9 developers, we can deduce that Scrum recommends the team size to be roughly 5-11 members. However, I decided to investigate this topic further as I was curious to how these numbers were derived. I studied the "Ringelmann Effect" which is a theory discovered by French agricultural engineer Maximilien Ringelmann. It concludes that members of a team will exert less effort when the size increases. In another study, the Ringelmann effect was re-examined. It confirmed the findings of the original study in which individual performance decreases after the addition of the first and second perceived worker but leveled off when a perceived group of 3-6 was added [15] Another study states that team size matters and that a large team size will result in social-loafing and reduced intra team communication.[15]

The International Software Benchmarking Standards Group (ISBSG) conducted a study and reported that there are three key factors that affect productivity in software development: programming language, development platform, and team size. They reported that team sizes equal to or greater than 9 are less productive than their smaller counterparts. [16]

In order to create a balanced argument for team size I tried researching for studies that were in favor for large team sizes. However, after conducting many queries, I couldn't find anything of substance. Based on the evidence that I gathered I can conclude that team sizes should be kept to a small number in order to maximize developers' productivity. This doesn't mean that a software company shouldn't hire hundreds of developers because if a company is big, like Microsoft for example, then they'll definitely need many developers. However, the developers should be placed into smaller teams.

# Chapter II Rewind

In this chapter you received a nice general overview of the Scrum framework. You learned about the central artifact in the framework which is the product backlog. Remember, the backlog is the ultimate to do list for a project and all of the requests are added to this single file. You then received a high-level overview of artifacts and events in Scrum. Artifacts represent the work the Scrum Team produce while events are key opportunities to inspect and adapt the process. Scrum is not a heavy-weight methodology but is instead a light-weight framework that can be molded and welded to fit the company that's implementing it. Lastly, you learned about the member roles in-and-outside the framework along with their main responsibilities. Understanding the team roles is critical because mixing and matching responsibilities will lead to unsatisfactory results. I like to refer to Scrum as a game that consists of team members and rules that they must follow in order to reach the goal which is producing quality increments of software.

# Chapter II Sources

1. Schwaber, Ken, and Jeff Sutherland. The Scrum Guide. July/August 2016. Accessed August 1, 2016. `http://www.scrumguides.org/docs/scrumguide/v2016/2016-Scrum-Guide-US.pdf`.

2. Beck, Kent, Mike Beedle, Arie Van Bennekum, Alistair Cockburn, Ward Cunningham, Martin Fowler, James Grenning, Jim Highsmith, Andrew Hunt, Ron Jeffries, Jon Kern, Brian Marick, Robert C. Martin, Steve Mellor, Ken Schwaber, Jeff Sutherland, and Dave Thomas. "Manifesto for Agile Software Development." Manifesto for Agile Software Development. 2001. Accessed August 01, 2016. `http://agilemanifesto.org`.

3. Illes-Seifert, Timea, and Barbara Paech. The Vital Few and Trivial Many: An Empirical Analysis of the Pareto Distribution of Defects. Accessed August 1, 2016. `http://subs.emis.de/LNI/Proceedings/Proceedings143/gi-proc-143-025.pdf`.

4. "The Zappos Founder Just Told Us All Kinds Of Crazy Stories – Here's The Surprisingly Candid Interview." The Business Insider. October/November, 2011. Accessed August 1, 2016. `http://www.businessinsider.com/nick-swinmurn-zappos-rnkd-2011-11`.

5. Cockburn, Alistair, and Laurie Williams. "The Costs and Benefits of Pair Programming" Accessed August 1, 2016. `http://collaboration.csc.ncsu.edu/laurie/Papers/XPSardinia.PDF`.

6. Coutu, Diane, and Carol Kauffman. "What Can Coaches Do for You?" Harvard Business Review. 2009. Accessed August 01, 2016. `https://hbr.org/2009/01/what-can-coaches-do-for-you`.

7. Valcour, Monique. "You Can't Be a Great Manager If You're Not a Good Coach." Harvard Business Review. 2014. Accessed August 01, 2016. `https://hbr.org/2014/07/you-cant-be-a-great-manager-if-youre-not-a-good-coach`.

8. Wendorff, Peter. "Coaching the Application of Agile Software Development." - Springer. Accessed August 01, 2007. http://link.springer.com/chapter/10.1007/978-0-387-72804-9_42.

9. Eisenbach, Regina, Kathleen Watson, and Rajnandin Pillai. "Transformational Leadership in the Context of Organizational Change." Accessed August 1, 2016. https://www.envisiongloballeadership.com/sites/default/files/pdf/Transformational leadership.pdf.

10. Costa, ML, Van L. Rensburg, and N. Rushton. "Does Teaching Style Matter? A Randomised Trial of Group Discussion versus Lectures in Orthopaedic Undergraduate Teaching." Pub Med, February 2007. Accessed August 1, 2016. http://www.ncbi.nlm.nih.gov/pubmed/17269956.

11. Karhatsu, Henri, Marko Ikonen, Petri Kettunen, and Fabian Fagerholm. "Building Blocks for Self-organizing Software Development Teams a Framework Model and Empirical Pilot Study." October/November 2010, 297-304. doi:10.1109/ICSTE.2010.5608848.

12. McDonough, Edward F., III. "Investigation of Factors Contributing to the Success of Cross-Functional Teams." Journal of Product Innovation Management, May/June, 2000, 221-35. Accessed August 1, 2016. doi:10.1016/S0737-6782(00)00041-2.

13. Baron, James N., and William T. Bielby. "The Proliferation of Job Titles in Organizations." Administrative Science Quarterly. Accessed August 1, 2016. doi:10.2307/2392964.

14. Ingham, Alan G., George Levinger, James Graves, and Vaugh Peckham. "The Ringelmann Effect: Studies of Group Size and Group Performance." Accessed August 1, 2016. doi:10.1016/0022-1031(74)90033-X.

15. Hoegl, Martin. Smaller Teams—better Teamwork: How to Keep Project Teams Small. Accessed August 1, 2016. http://www.managementcheck.de/Downloads/Research Studies/HOEGL_Business_Horizons_2005.pdf.

16. "Team Size Impacts Special Report." http://isbsg.org/product/team-size-impacts-special-report.

# Chapter II Quiz

## GENERAL SCRUM QUESTIONS

1. **According to the Scrum Guide which of the following are true?**

   a) The product backlog is the ONLY source of requirements that the Dev Team are allowed to work from

   b) The ENTIRE organization must respect the Product Owner's decisions

   c) The Dev Team can't act on what anyone else says EXCEPT the CEO of the company

   d) The Product Owner is one person that represents the desires of many

2. **Company XYZ has a Scrum Team called "No Bug Left Behind." The team consists of 6 developers in which two of them handle testing duties. One of the two testers had an unexpected event and left in the midst of the project. What should the team do? Select the BEST answer.**

   a) Reduce the amount of tasks they're working on since their numbers are less

   b) Self-organize and apply the principles of cross-functionality to make up the workload

   c) Consult the Product Owner so that they can add a temporary contractual developer

   d) Continue working as normal as they have an intricate plan

3. **What's the relationship between empirical process control and agility? Select the BEST answer.**

   a) Agile is a subset of the empirical process control

   b) Agile has 3 rules like the empirical process control

   c) It requires Agile to understand how to improve software

   d) There's no relationship

4. **How many events are there in Scrum?**

    a) 2
    b) 3
    c) 4
    d) 5

5. **True or False?: Once a person has achieved a Scrum certification they have become an expert in Scrum.**

6. **Which of the following is the best definition of Scrum?**

    a) A methodology for developing quality software by the application of sophisticated software engineering techniques
    b) A loose framework for managing the development of complex products
    c) A set of heuristics for iteratively and incrementally building quality software
    d) A complete system for managing software development

# TEAM ROLES

7. **Select all of the following statements that are true about the Product Owner (PO):**

    a) The PO is considered a key stakeholder as they have keen interests in the commercial success of the project
    b) The PO shouldn't be confused with a traditional product manager
    c) The product manager manages the entire project, while the PO manages the product backlog
    d) They work closely with key stakeholders to ensure that the project is being completed accurately and timely

8. **All of the following are true about the Product Owner except?**

    a) They help clarify any ambiguities about the backlog items to the Dev Team
    b) They're responsible for making sure that the backlog is accessible to everyone
    c) They're the only ones that can order the backlog items
    d) They're responsible for organizing the backlog so that it achieves maximum value

9. **Select all of the following that are true about the Product Owner:**

   **a)** They're responsible for maximizing the value of the work the Dev Team produces

   **b)** The way the Product Owner maximizes value across organizations is the same

   **c)** The Product Owner and the Dev Team collaborate on building the backlog and are both responsible for its management

   **d)** The Product Owner prioritizes the backlog by weight

10. **Which of the following is the Product Owner's Responsibility regarding the backlog? Select all that apply.**

    **a)** Its order

    **b)** Its content

    **c)** Its availability

    **d)** Its estimates

11. **Which of the following are true about the Scrum Master's role? Select all that apply.**

    **a)** They're considered the enforcer of Scrum for the team

    **b)** They're considered a servant-leader

    **c)** They help the Scrum Team become cross-functional and self-organizing

    **d)** They understand and practice the rules of Agile

12. **Select all of the following that are true about the Scrum Master:**

    **a)** They should work with other Scrum Masters within the organization to increase the application of Scrum

    **b)** They help coordinate Scrum implementations in the organization

    **c)** They coach other Scrum Masters in the organization

    **d)** None of the above is true

13. **Select all of the following that are true about the Scrum Master:**

    **a)** Makes sure that The Scrum Team follow Scrum rules

    **b)** Makes sure that The Scrum Team follow Scrum theory

    **c)** Makes sure that The Scrum Team follow Scrum practices

    **d)** Makes sure that The Scrum Team follow Scrum methodologies

**14. Select all of the following that's true about the Scrum Master**

- **a)** They serve the Dev Team
- **b)** They help the Dev Team facilitate events
- **c)** They help the Dev Team produce high-value software
- **d)** They help the Dev Team refine the product backlog

**15. Select all of the following that are true regarding the Scrum Master**

- **a)** Helps the organization as a whole adapt Scrum
- **b)** Helps the company CEO understand Scrum
- **c)** Disrupt the current ecosystem of the workplace to induce productivity
- **d)** Help the stakeholders understand empirical process control

**16. Select all of the following that are true about the Scrum Master**

- **a)** Facilitates the prescribed events in Scrum
- **b)** Coaches the Dev Team on better coding practices
- **c)** Eliminates obstacles that are slowing down the Dev Team's progress
- **d)** Coaches developers from non-Scrum environments on how to adapt Scrum

**17. Select all of the following that are true about the Scrum Master**

- **a)** They inform those outside the team which interactions were helpful
- **b)** They inform those outside the team which interactions were not helpful
- **c)** They help change interactions to maximize value created by Scrum Team
- **d)** They maximize the value of the backlog

**18. The Scrum Guide mentions that the Scrum Master is responsible for understanding product planning in an empirical environment. Which of the following options BEST explains this concept?**

- **a)** The Scrum Master needs to create static plans that adhere to the goal of the organization
- **b)** The Scrum Master should have excellent planning skills
- **c)** The Scrum Master must know how to time-box and plan schedules accordingly
- **d)** The Scrum Master must be able to adjust plans during the project's duration

19. **What happens when multiple Dev Teams work on the same product? Select all that apply.**
    a) They're guaranteed to get the project done quicker
    b) Multiple teams with varying development times may make it hard to synchronize work
    c) The same amount of work will most likely get done during the first development cycle
    d) According to University published studies this will ironically cause the project to be delayed

20. **Select all of the following that are true about the Dev Team**
    a) They have all the skill-sets needed to complete the job
    b) They decide how they complete work
    c) They're either self-organizing or cross-functional
    d) They must complete an increment of product with each development cycle

21. **Select all of the following that are true about the Dev Team.**
    a) They're typically small with no more than 9 developers
    b) Some small teams can have skill constraints
    c) Smaller teams tend to be more flexible and thus more agile
    d) Having a large Dev Team could make applying empirical process control difficult

22. **Select all of the following that are true about the Dev Team.**
    a) They build the software
    b) They're self-organizing
    c) They consist of developers that also handle testing
    d) Since they're cross-functional there are no specialized skills

23. **Select all of the following that are true about The Dev Team.**
    a) A business analyst is a role in Scrum, and they are part of The Dev Team
    b) It's okay to have sub-teams within The Dev Team
    c) A Dev Team should have testers
    d) The Dev Team can adapt to changing requirements

24. **Select all of the following that are true about The Dev Team.**
    a) They must create a product increment by the end of the development cycle

b) Since the Dev Team is self-organizing they don't listen to anyone outside of it

c) Since the Dev Team should be cross-functional, this implies that every developer should have the skills of the other

d) The Product Owner empowers The Dev Team to manage their work

### 25. Select all of the following that are true about The Dev Team in Scrum?

a) There's a senior developer in every Scrum Team

b) There are more than 2 developers each Scrum Team

c) The developers of a Scrum Team can only work on ONE product at a time

d) Since developers are self-organized there's no structure

### 26. The Product Owner is responsible for managing which of the following?

a) Product Backlog

b) Accounting for the company

c) Risk

d) The Development Team

### 27. The team structure in Scrum is designed to optimize which of the following? Select all that apply.

a) Flexibility

b) Manageability

c) Creativity

d) Productivity

### 28. Which Scrum role is responsible for managing the Product Backlog?

a) Product Owner

b) Product Owner + Scrum Master

c) Product Owner + Dev Team

d) Everyone

### 29. Which team role is responsible for ensuring that events are held?

a) Product Owner

b) Scrum Master

c) Dev Team

d) Everyone

30. **Select all of the following that are true about The Scrum Team**
    a) They work iteratively and incrementally
    b) They maximize chances for feedback
    c) They figure out how to best develop the product increment
    d) Product Owner, Scrum Master, Dev Team, and stakeholders are all part of the team.

31. **True or False: According to the Scrum Guide even though the Dev Team have the jurisdiction to select how they do work, the C-Suite executives like the company CEO can override their decisions if they feel it's for the greater good of the company.**

32. **True or False: The Scrum Master should be well-versed in strategies on how to get the team to quickly respond to change.**

33. **True or False: The Product Owner is responsible for creating the Sprint Goal.**

34. **True or False: The Scrum Team collaborates as a whole during Sprint Planning.**

35. **True or False: A Scrum Master can never be part of the Dev Team.**

36. **True or False: A Product Owner can never be part of the Dev Team.**

37. **True or False: The Dev Team typically starts out designing the system and the product backlog items.**

38. **True or False: If the work The Dev Team produces during a Sprint turns out to be different than they expected, they can collaborate with the Product Owner to negotiate the scope of the Sprint Backlog.**

39. **True or False: A Project Manager is the same as a Product Owner.**

40. **True or False: The Product Owner is essentially the same as a Product Manager?**

41. True or False: The Scrum Master serves the Product Owner, Development Team, and entire organization.

42. True or False: The Scrum Master coaches only the Product Owner and Scrum Team.

43. True or False: To maximize efficiency The Dev Team should only reserve self-organizing to when they design and develop software.

44. True or False: There can be multiple Product Owners for a product if the scope of the project is too large for one Product Owner to handle.

45. True or False: Scrum Teams are small in order to maximize communication and productivity.

# PRODUCT BACKLOG QUESTIONS

46. Select all of the following that are true about the Product Backlog?
    a) Effective prioritization of it is important for the success of the team
    b) The most important features should be given a higher prominence
    c) The Product Owner's decision is transparent to the team through its content and ordering
    d) In order to change a backlog item's priority the Product Owner must be consulted

47. Which one of the following is TRUE about Product Backlog?
    a) Scrum projects don't use them
    b) They're owned by the Scrum Master
    c) It's a Scrum artifact
    d) They're owned by the Dev Team

48. Select all of the following that are true about the Product Backlog.
    a) Changes in technology can cause it to mutate
    b) Changes in the marketplace can cause it to mutate

**c)** Multiple teams can work on the same backlog

**d)** Its considered a LIVING artifact

### 49. All of the following are recommended to be added to the Product Backlog Items except?

**a)** Description

**b)** Estimate

**c)** Order

**d)** Cost

### 50. As a product is released to the market and gains feedback, which of the following most likely happens to the backlog?

**a)** It stays the same

**b)** It decreases

**c)** It increases

**d)** None of the above

### 51. What's the maximum number of backlogs that can be available for a product?

**a)** 1

**b)** 2

**c)** 3

**d)** 4

### 52. Which one of the following is TRUE about Product Backlog?

**a)** The backlog will stay until the completion of the termination of the product

**b)** It's always changing

**c)** The Product Owner prioritizes the items in the backlog

**d)** The Dev Team orders the items by importance

### 53. Which of the following is true about the ordering of the Product Backlog?

**a)** The Development Team only orders it

**b)** The Scrum Master orders it

**c)** It's ordered randomly

**d)** It depends

### 54. True or False: The Product Backlog should contain all product features. This includes functions, requirements, enhancements and fixes.

55. **True or False: A Product Backlog only exists for products that have not been released into the market.**

56. **True or False: The Product Backlog vanishes after the product is released into the market.**

# TEAM SIZE QUESTIONS

57. **If a company has 5 products on the market then how many backlogs will they have? Select the BEST answer.**
    a) 1
    b) 3
    c) 5
    d) None of the above

58. **What's the range for developers allowed on a Scrum Team?**
    a) 6 3 3
    b) 3 3 9
    c) 2 3 7
    d) There's no limit as it varies by team

59. **Company XYZ has a Scrum Team called "Problem Busters" that have a Product Owner, Scrum Master, and Dev Team—they have 10 names on the whiteboard. The company CEO who has a close relationship with the team looked at the employees' profiles on the private company forum and noticed only 8 names. Why is this case? Select the BEST answer.**
    a) This was a typographical error
    b) The Scrum Master and Product Owner are also on the Dev Team
    c) Two members got fired
    d) None of the above

60. **This question continues from question 59. How many developers are on team "Problem Busters?" Select the BEST answer.**
    a) 6
    b) 8
    c) At most 3
    d) Impossible to tell

61. **Company XYZ has 12 products in their portfolio. What's the minimum number of developers they can staff? (HINT: Assume that there is 1 team dedicated to each product)**

   **a)** 9
   **b)** 36
   **c)** 48
   **d)** 54

62. **This question continues from question 61. A year later company XYZ expanded and released two more products and now has a total of 14 products in their portfolio. What's the maximum number of developers the company can staff according to The Scrum Guide? (HINT: Assume that there is 1 team dedicated to each product)**

   **a)** 14
   **b)** 100
   **c)** 126
   **d)** 154

63. **True or False: A main drawback of large teams is that it makes applying the empirical process control difficult.**

# Chapter II Answers

## GENERAL SCRUM QUESTIONS

1. Choices (a), (b), and (d) are correct. According to Scrum Guide the backlog is the official source of requirements and the developers are not permitted to act on what anyone else says.

2. Choice (b). In an ideal situation The Dev Team should have an understanding of each other's work just in case something unexpected happens so that they can re-adjust without disrupting the work flow significantly. Choice (c) may sound appropriate but according to the book "The Mythical Man Month" authored by Fred Brooks, adding resources to an already late project delays it further.

3. Choice (c). The empirical process control relies on transparency, inspect, and adaption in order to improve software. These elements are components of Agile so in order to understand empirical process you must understand the concepts of Agile.

4. Choice (d). The five events are: Sprint Planning, Daily Scrum, Sprint, Sprint Review, and Sprint Retrospective.

5. False. Scrum certifications are good for testing general knowledge, kind of like a driving license tests someone's general knowledge of driving on the road. However, a person truly masters Scrum through its application in a real world environment.

6. Choice (b) only. Scrum can be classified as a framework for building complex products. Frameworks are not rigid so therefore could

be considered loose. Even though it's typically used in software development its application is versatile as it has been applied to a myriad of industries like finance, education, and government.

## TEAM ROLES

7. All of the options are true. Refer to the section about the Product owner role in Chapter II.

8. Choice (c). The Dev Team with the approval of the Product Owner is allowed to make changes to the product backlog. Refer to the team roles section in Chapter II for additional details.

9. Choice (a). The way the PO maximizes value across organizations will vary, and while the PO and Dev Team may collaborate on managing the backlog, the PO is responsible for it. Lastly, the Product Owner prioritizes the backlog by value.

10. Choices (a), (b), and (c) are correct. While they help clarify any doubts, they don't estimate the backlog items as that's a job that the Dev Team is responsible for.

11. All of the following are the responsibilities of The Scrum Master. Refer to the team roles section in Chapter II for further clarification.

12. Choices (a), (b), and (c) are correct. If there's multiple Scrum Teams then there will be multiple Scrum Masters who can continually educate each other about correctly implementing Scrum within the organization. Refer to the team roles section in Chapter II for further clarification.

13. Choices (a), (b), and (c) are correct. Since Scrum is a framework there are no methodologies so option (d) is invalid.

14. Choices (a), (b), and (c) are true. Choice (d) is incorrect as this is something that the Dev Team does with the assistance of the Product Owner.

15. All of these options are correct. Refer to the team roles section in Chapter II for further clarification.

16. Choices (a), (c), and (d) are correct. Choice (b) is incorrect as the Scrum Master doesn't coach the Dev Team on using better practices but instead coach them on how to apply Scrum.

17. Choices (a), (b), and (c) are correct. One of the Scrum Master's duties includes helping those outside the team understand which of their interactions were and weren't helpful to the Scrum Team. They do this with the intention of maximizing the value that the Scrum Team creates. Refer to the team roles section in Chapter II for further clarification.

18. Choice (d). Empiricism implies that the process is based from experience which means that action must be taken and results should be analyzed to improve subsequent cycles. This type of environment experience changes which is something that the Scrum Team will have to account for.

19. Choice (b). Although (a) seems reasonable it's not guaranteed. Multiple teams working together means more overhead to manage which could cause a delay in early cycles but convert into quicker releases in the future if the process is optimized.

20. Choice (a), (b), and (d) are true. The Dev Team MUST is self-organizing AND cross-functional which makes choice (c) incorrect.

21. All of the above are true.

22. Choices (a), (b), and (c) are true. There could be developers with specialized skills in Scrum but they still have a shared accountability for the product increment.

23. Choices (c) and (d). A business analyst is a role in traditional project management but Scrum doesn't prescribe a role for them.

24. Choice (c) only. The Dev Team should strive to create a releasable product increment at the end of the development cycle, but it's not a must. Also, the Dev Team should be receptive to feedback in order to continually improve their process.

25. Choices (b) and (c) are correct. The Dev Team in Scrum ranges from 3-9 developers. There are no specific titles for the developers

in Scrum and since they're cross-functional they must have multiple skill-sets. The Dev Team is self-organizing but it's still structured in order to maximize chances of producing a product increment by the end of each development cycle.

26. Choices (a) and (c). While knowledge of finances and accounting may assist a Product Owner in their role, book-keeping is not their responsibility. Also, the Product Owner doesn't manage any team member as a Scrum Team is self-organizing.

27. Choices (a), (c), and (d). Scrum empowers the team members meaning that they make decisions on how things get done.

28. Choice (a). The Product Owner collaborates with the Scum Team to augment the backlog, but they're the ones responsible for it.

29. Choice (b). The Scrum Master is responsible for making sure that events occur and are time-boxed.

30. Choices (a), (b), and (c) are correct. Choice (d) is incorrect because stakeholders are not part of the actual Scrum Team.

31. False. According to the Scrum Guide self-organizing teams have control over how they get work done and they're not allowed to listen to anyone else regarding this.

32. True. According to The Scrum Guide the Scrum Master should be knowledgeable in agility, and quickly responding to change is an aspect of it.

33. False. The entire Scrum Team crafts the Sprint Goal.

34. True. This is especially important so that all team members understand the objectives for the upcoming Sprint.

35. False: It's generally not recommended but they can be if needed.

36. False. It's generally not recommended but they can be if needed.

37. True. This is typically the process that most Dev Teams implement before proceeding to build the product increment.

38. True. Negotiating is allowed in Scrum even during a Sprint.

39. False. The job description of a project manager can be defined as someone that generally plans, orchestrates, and finish products in accordance to their requirements and deadline. This role is generally more encompassing than a Product Owner whose primary focus is managing the product backlog. Depending on the industry for example project managers could be responsible for bringing in personnel from different departments such as marketing and finance.

40. False: In traditional project management a project manager is the individual responsible for leading a project from its inception through execution. While a Product Owner in Scrum may share some of attributes of a traditional project manager the main distinction is a PO focuses on the product backlog—a project manager is involved in the overall management of the entire project.

41. True. As the Scrum Guide states, the Scrum Master is a servant-leader that serves the Scrum Team and the organization.

42. False. They also coach the entire organization on how to adapt Scrum.

43. False. They can self-organize during the project lifecycle.

44. False. According to the Scrum Guide there's 1 Product Owner per each product. If the PO is having difficulties with managing the backlog then they can discuss these issues with the Scrum Team and stakeholders.

45. True. Refer back to the section in Chapter II that discuss team sizes.

## PRODUCT BACKLOG QUESTIONS

46. All of these options are correct.

47. Choice (c). It's a Scrum artifact. They're three artifacts in Scrum which are Product Backlog, Sprint Backlog, and Increment.

48. All of these are correct. Refer to the Product Backlog Mastery section in Chapter II for further details.

49. Choice (d). Cost is not something that appears on a PBI. Instead, value is used to denote how useful an item is to the entire product.

50. Choice (c). It most likely increases in size as customers request additional features or discover bugs that need to be patched.

51. Choice (a). The Product Backlog is the single source for all requirements or changes that needs to be made. There can only be one backlog per product. However, to help delegate tasks Scrum Teams can categorize the items.

52. Choice (d). This is something that the Product Owner does.

53. Choice (d). The Scrum Guide doesn't explicitly specify how it's ordered, but it does say that the Product Owner is responsible for its ordering, availability, and content.

54. True. According to the Scrum Guide all of these components of the product should be listed in the backlog.

55. False. The Product Backlog will last as long until the product is removed from the market. If a product stays on the market for years then more than likely it will need to be updated in order stay relevant to their customers.

56. False. It's alive until the product is removed from the market.

## TEAM SIZE QUESTIONS

57. Choice (c). Since every product gets an associated backlog there'll be five backlogs total.

58. Choice (a). There are 3-9 developers allowed on a Scrum team. Refer back to the section in Chapter II regarding team size for additional clarification.

59. Choice (b). The question states that the company has 1 SM, 1 PO, and a Dev Team—it mentions that there are 10 names on the whiteboard but never said that they were all unique. Since the company CEO has a close relationship with the Scrum Team they would most likely knew if two team members were fired so we can deduce that the SM and PO are also on The Dev Team.

60. Choice (b). We knew from the previous question that the Scrum Team has a total of 8 members and we also knew that the Scrum Master and Product Owner are also on the Dev Team. Therefore, we can conclude that there are a total of 8 developers.

61. Choice (b). According to Scrum there are a minimum of 3 developers needed per Scrum Team, so 3 x 12 equates to the minimum of 36 developers that needs to be staffed.

62. Choice (c). The Scrum Guide recommends setting a boundary of 9 developers max per Scrum Team. Therefore, if a company has 14 teams with the maximum number of developers allowed then the result would be 14 x 9 or 126 developers.

63. True. According to The Scrum Guide having more than 9 team members makes managing the empirical process control complex.

# CHAPTER III:

# Planning Phase

This chapter covers the components of Scrum that take place prior to actual development. Building quality software could be a difficult task, therefore to maximize the team's chances of shipping defect-free software on time careful planning must be done beforehand.

# Sprint Planning

The **Sprint Planning** meeting is a mastermind session in which the Scrum Team congregates to brainstorm how they'll work together to deliver a shippable product by the end of the upcoming Sprint. Like all events in Scrum, it is time-boxed to ensure that the team doesn't expend too many resources. The maximum amount of time a team can use for a 4-week Sprint is 8-hours, for Sprints of a smaller length it's a shorter duration. Scrum adapts the Agile mindset which means that the team executes an $n$ amount of micro-planning sessions over the duration of the project. As more Sprint cycles are executed the requirements for the project should become more lucid. The entire Scrum team collaborates to create the plan. The Scrum Master is the team member that orchestrates this event and ensures that everyone understands its purpose. They also make sure that the team keeps the Sprint Planning session within the allocated time-box. There are two primary questions which emerge during Sprint Planning which are, what can be done, and how will the work get done?  It's difficult for the team to formulate a plan for building a shippable product increment at the end of the upcoming Sprint without answering these questions.

## WHAT CAN BE DELIVERED IN THE UPCOMING SPRINT?

The Dev Team have complete jurisdiction over the what, and how things get done for the upcoming Sprint. This in theory means that even the company CEO can't tell the Dev Team how to do their work. This concept is in alignment with self-organization in which power is delegated to the Dev Team to complete work. The Dev Team is given a couple of components to start-off with to assist them in determining the appropriate workload. Some inputs are the product backlog, forecasted capacity, past performance, and latest product increment. A team that hasn't completed one Sprint yet will have less to work with—all they will have is the product backlog and the forecasted capacity of the team. As mentioned previously the product backlog is most unstable in the early stages of the project as this is when the organization knows less about the product that they're trying to build. The second variable is the forecasted capacity of the team which is also not hyper-reliable in the early stages. There are however some consensus making strategies that they can use to help get closer to the *sweet spot* when predicting the workload they can handle in the upcoming Sprint which I discuss in the Estimation Strategies section later on in this chapter. After the Dev Team chooses the backlog items that they can handle during the Sprint they devise a goal for the upcoming Sprint, known as the Sprint Goal.

# SPRINT GOAL

The Sprint Goal is the purpose of the upcoming Sprint. There should only be one goal per-Sprint as having several of them is hard to manage and could cause the team to be unfocused. This doesn't mean that the Scrum Team should only do one thing per-Sprint because that's not the case. Instead, it means that the backlog items that the team selects each Sprint should bind together for a common purpose. The Sprint Goal should be specific to make the objectives clear. Having a Sprint Goal of complete all of the user-stories for a Sprint seems ideal on paper but is inherently specious—just missing one user-story will cause the Sprint Goal to fail even if the team delivered exceptional value to the customer. Therefore, it's better to create well-defined user-stories. The explicit Sprint Goal will assist the team in understanding why they're building the Increment. According to the Scrum Guide, the Sprint Goal can also be something that causes the team to work together rather than separately. Therefore, pair-programming can be included with a Sprint Goal as it causes the team to collaborate. Once the Dev Team enters the Sprint Cycle they'll build code with the Sprint Goal as their "North Star. " If they determine that they miscalculated their capacity for the Sprint then they consult with the PO to modify the scope of the work.

## HOW WILL THE WORK GET DONE?

Once the Dev Team selects the backlog items and the Scrum Team collectively forms the Sprint Goal, the next step is for the Dev Team to decide how they'll get the work done. In this stage who, what, and how the work gets done is answered. A typical method that's used to represent backlog items in Agile is user-stories which will be elaborated later on in this chapter. During this stage the stories are decomposed into tasks or units of work for the first couple of days of the upcoming Sprint. The team can decide to breakdown the entire backlog if it's something that they can handle within the time box. The team self-organizes to determine who's in charge for completing what, management is not involved. The Dev Team typically starts off by implementing a loose design. Since agile projects are highly unstable, implementing a tight-design could be an expensive development mistake down the road when changes are likely to happen. Therefore, building flexibility into the design for a new project is a sage decision to combat the dilemma of uncertainty.

The PO should be there to provide expert advice or eradicate any confusion about the backlog items. After the Dev Team has conducted their estimates for the selected backlog items, they may re-negotiate the work that gets done with the PO. They can petition to reduce the amount of user-stories completed during a Sprint if they believe they can't complete all of them, or they can conversely request the addition of backlog items if they feel that the workload is too low. The PO should be there to provide any guidance to the Dev Team and answer any questions that they may have about estimating the workload. It's critical that the PO and the Dev Team collaborates intensely when deriving estimates. If the Dev Team is uncertain about providing accurate estimates then they can bring in consultants to assist them with deriving accurate estimates. By the end of this session they should be able to communicate to the Scrum Team how they plan to self-organize in order to obtain the Sprint Goal and produce a shippable Increment.

# SPRINT BACKLOG

The last phase to the Spring Planning session is to construct the Sprint Backlog. This is an artifact in Scrum that's derived by combining the Sprint Goal, selected backlog items, and plan for implementation. In layman terms the **Sprint Backlog** can be considered a derivative of the Product Backlog that contains predictions for the workload needed to produce a shippable product Increment by the end of the Sprint. The Sprint Backlog should be transparent to the entire Scrum

Team as it contains the blueprint for what the team is going to be working on next. The Sprint Backlog like the Product Backlog is not immutable, and will constantly be undergoing fluctuations throughout the course of the project. The Dev Team will constantly add, remove, and update items in the Sprint Backlog. The Dev Team has complete jurisdiction over the Sprint Backlog.

# INCREMENT

The Increment is the accumulation of all the product backlog items completed during the recent Sprint, along with the past ones. The team must devise a "Definition of Done" (DoD) which verifies that the Increment was produced to the team's standard. The Increment must be stable and be in useable condition regardless if the PO plans to ship it or not. By having Increments that are not useable means that the team is accumulating waste and are not adhering to the principles of Agile which is working software.

# Estimation Strategies

According to the Merriam-Webster dictionary an *estimate* is *the process in which a general idea about value, size, or cost is formed*. Accurate software estimation is important for the success of a project for several reasons. One, it helps the team stay on track towards reaching a goal. Two, it helps the executives sponsoring the project to gauge the costs for it. Lastly, accurate software estimates could help prolong the tenure of the project. However, delivering accurate estimates is a notorious conundrum in the software realm, especially for new products. A stable product that has been on the market for a decade is a well-oiled machine and has resolved many of the unprecedented variables that it came across. The team has become the master over the product and is in a much better position to provide accurate estimates for future endeavors. However, getting to this stage is not a bed of roses, and generating accurate estimates for large, complex software projects can become a demystifying puzzle to inexperienced Scrum Teams. The good news is that the foundations for estimating the complexity of software features have been researched for decades and I plan to transfer this knowledge to you in this section.

## STORY POINTS

A **story point** is as an arbitrary unit that describes the complexity of completing a user-story. Story points are not synonymous with man-hours. The reasoning for using an arbitrary unit is because humans are not innate with providing absolute estimates. For example, if someone were to ask you to describe how tall the building you lodge in is, you more than likely won't be able to provide an accurate estimate. However, if someone asks you to compare the size of the building to a nearby one, you'll more than likely be able to tell if it's taller, shorter, or equal to it. Providing relative estimates is what humans are better at and mastering this concept can help developers gain higher insights into the complexity of their projects.

Let's take a look at example STORY POINTS. Let's say that company XYZ has taken on a new project. The user-stories are broken down by the Product Owner and then handed to the Dev Team for estimates. Let's assume that the company is working on developing a Kernel program and thus decides to use the C-language to build it. For "Story A" Developer 1 provides an estimate of 3-hours to complete it since they have 10+ years of experience with C and have worked on a similar program before. However, Developer 2 who is fresh out of college has no experience with C outside of a college course that they mostly sleep-walked through. They estimated that this feature will take them at least 8-hours to complete. Which developer estimate is accurate? This is a trick question because they both are. When you bring a team of developers together some will be more experienced than others. Therefore, estimating in hours can initially be unstable as some developers will be able to complete tasks faster than others. An advantage with using story points is that both developers can report the same difficulty regardless of their experience. Going back to i.e. STORY POINTS, if company XYZ decides to adapt story points instead of man-hours, then Developer 1 could report that Story A have a difficulty of 3 story points, and Developer 2 could also report that it has a difficulty of 3 story points.

Remember, story points are a relative basis of measurement not an absolute one. Two different developers can report the same number for a story but still take different times in completing them. An analogous example outside of the development world is running the mile. It's possible for two in-shape adults to report the difficulty of running a mile on a scale of 1-10—both runners could report the difficulty of completing the mile as a 4, but one runner could complete it quicker than the other. To build upon i.e. STORY POINTS, in order for developers to increase the accuracy of their estimates it's critical that they have an example story that they can use as their baseline. I prefer to use simple stories for this as that's the one that the team can generally form a quick consensus on. If the baseline story has a story point of one, then Developer 1 and 2 can use it as a benchmark to confirm the accuracy of Story A which should be roughly 3 times the complexity. If it's not then they should re-evaluate their estimates as there's deviation somewhere. Forming an accurate baseline is critical to ensure that the team is providing the right estimates with their story points—otherwise the team is in essence making wild guesses which is akin to gambling with the company's resources. This method of using a baseline to verify the accuracy of estimates is known as *triangulation*. Once the team has estimated several backlog items they could select several reference stories of varying sizes to expedite the estimation process.

# MAN HOURS

This is one of the most basic units that companies use to measure employees' productivity. A man-hour can be defined as the amount of work a single employee can complete within 60-minutes. This is the type of unit that customers like to request when they're asking for turnaround times. For example, if a software development company charges $100 per hour, and they estimate that to deliver the final product according to the buyer's terms in 75 man-hours, then they'll quote the company at $7500. This type of strategy is OK if the company has a history of doing a manual repeatable process like manufacturing a Bentwood Chair. However, this line of work is drastically different from building a software program as domain knowledge may be unknown making estimations difficult. One of the best ways for a company to get better at providing accurate estimates is through experience. If they have successfully completed many products then there's a higher chance that related concepts will manifest in future products. My advice is don't commit to work that you can't deliver on-time because that will lead to managerial complications. Teams should constantly practice providing estimates in order to build their accuracy. It's not illogical to assume that smaller tasks will derive more accurate estimates due to there being less room for uncertainties. Therefore, it's recommended for Scrum Teams to breakdown stories further into tasks and then provide estimates in terms of man-hours. Tasks can be described as features that can be completed within one workday.

# STORY POINTS VS. MAN HOURS FAQS

**QUESTION:** I'm still confused. Which one should my Scrum Team use? Story points or man-hours?

**ANSWER:** It's quite confusing in the beginning. Some *Agilest* are proponents of using story points for high-level planning and man-hours for low-level tasks and I tend to agree with this philosophy. However, remember that the team has the right to self-organize, and that includes selecting which method they use to determine estimates. If they choose to use story points only, or man-hours only, then their decision should be respected as long as they provide their reasoning.

**QUESTION:** What's the main difference between story points and man-hours?

**ANSWER:** Story points are an abstraction unit while man-hours are explicit. I would advise against mixing story points with man-hours in the beginning stages since they're different units of measurements. For example, inches and centimeters are both units for measuring the length of an object, but mixing them together could lead to inaccurate measurements or less proper conversions are done. The difficulty with mixing story points and man-hours together is that there's no standardization hence conversions are not possible across all software teams. It's a known fact that 1-inch is equivalent to 2.54 centimeters which makes converting from centimeters to inches and vice-versa straightforward. However, this is not the case with mixing story points and man-hours. The reason being is that for the same story "Team A" may give it a story point of 3, and Team B may do the same. However, Team A may complete the story in 10 man-hours while Team B may do it in 5 man-hours. Remember, all teams consist of different individuals with unique experience levels, and therefore will vary in the speed of completing work. Since story points are a relative measure two teams can report the same story point measurement but in reality complete the story at varying speeds. While I would advise against generalizing story points across teams I'm not against generalizing story points within a team. After the team has completed several iterations of development they'll have a deeper understanding of the sphere of the project through a combination of research and experience. In matter of fact, there's a research study that analyzed undergraduate students placed in Scrum Teams for a software engineering course. As the project progressed the Scrum Teams became better at planning their work for subsequent Sprints, and by the third one the velocity stabilized. [1]

While case studies are nice to reference they shouldn't be used as a silver-bullet, but more of a baseline to expand upon. The real determiner in the team's stability is their past experience. The more development cycles a team of the same developers have undergone the more reliable their past capacity becomes. In short, immature teams estimates are more likely to be unreliable compared to mature teams—the common denominator that mature teams have is time working together.

**QUESTION:** How can a team finish projects timely if one developer is much slower than another? For example, Developer 1 provides an estimate for task ABC as 2-hours, while Developer 2 estimates the same task as 8-hours.

**ANSWER:** This is an inherent problem that most development teams will face sooner or later. However, the good news is that there's a relatively straight-forward solution to this issue that has been around for decades. The solution is connected to the manufacturing process in *Kanban*. When a bottleneck arises and slows down the entire production process, the team stops as a whole and commit their resources to alleviating the bottleneck known as *swarming*. Once the bottleneck is resolved the team resumes their individual tasks. In terms of software development the technical bottleneck can be alleviated by pairing the inexperienced developer with the more experience one also known as pair-programming. This diffuses information sharing and increases cross-functionality. However, in order for this to work the more experienced developer must be willing to commit their time to bringing the less experienced one up to speed. If they don't have any empathy then most likely the team will struggle. In addition, if the more experienced developer commits too much of their time then they'll also run behind schedule, so a delicate balance should be in place.

**QUESTION:** How can a team of developers provide accurate estimates for technology they're not familiar with?

**ANSWER:** It's asking the developer to do something very difficult. Anyone can provide an estimate, but the value manifests when the estimate is accurate. When a developer provides an estimate for 4-hours, one should not assume that the developer sits at their desk, loads up an IDE, and codes for 4-hours straight until the desired outcome is reached. There's a lot of implicit cognition that the developer does like acquiring knowledge about an unfamiliar domain which should all be calculated into the estimate. If a team is completely unfamiliar with a domain then Scrum does grant the Dev Team the right to bring in other people to provide technical advice.

**QUESTION:** Why can't developers eliminate estimates?

**ANSWER:** In short, it's beneficial to the developers but not to the sponsors paying for the project. One of the values of the Agile Manifesto is customer collaboration over contract negotiation. [2] In a new project there's a lot at stake, and if the Dev Team are unwilling to provide estimates then the sponsor will more than likely find another company that will. It's an uncomfortable position for developers because the early stages of a project is critical as that's when contracts are typically won, but ironically that's when developers know the least about the domain of the project. My advice is for each developer on the team to know their limits, and for the team as a whole to understand their strengths and weaknesses. If the customer is asking for the team to deliver a large amount of software in a time that the team have estimated that's virtually impossible then they can collaborate with the customer and educate them about the philosophy of Scrum. One of the selling points of this framework is that companies can get small increments of useable product shipped to them in 1-4 weeks. They don't have to wait until 12 dreaded months to receive everything in one-shot, but can instead get smaller portions of the product until it completes the whole. If the customer finds value in this then the original contract can be re-negotiated and the Dev Team can now work within reasonable time constraints.

# TEAM DECISION MAKING

Group estimation is an important concept in Agile based methods. After all, one of the values in agile is that the most effective method of conveying information within a development team is by face-to-face conversation. [2]

The Dev Team needs to rely on each other in order to increase their chances of obtaining the Sprint Goal. It's no secret that groups produce significantly higher-quality products than individuals. [3]

Therefore it's crucial that the Scrum Team collaborates and makes decisions as a unit is as opposed to individually. In this section

I present two popular methods for group consensus decision making in detail. It's recommended to experiment with these methods to see which one fits better with your team.

# PLANNING POKER

(c) www.purcellconsult.com

*Figure 3.1: Planning poker*

Planning poker is a gamification strategy used by Dev Teams to estimate the *size* of a user-story. The size could indicate how long it takes, its difficulty, or expense—the unit of measurement is a variable that the team decides. In order to provide a thorough explanation of Planning Poker I'm going to provide a counter-example and illustrate unstructured group decision making.

1) Product Owner asks Dev Team to estimate user-story "Headache" in ideal man-hours.

2) The team of four developers start to think about their estimates.

**3)** Developer α (alpha) who's the most experienced developer selects a 5 from the deck and boastfully states: "this story shouldn't take any more than 5-hours max. It's a genetic algorithm which I have plenty of experience with."

**4)** Developer β (beta) and ι (iota) are both rookie developers that never worked with genetic algorithms and they start second-guessing their original estimates due to α comment. Developer ω (omega) who tends to overestimate user-stories decides to give it a 40. Developer α is adamant that his choice is correct and decides for the team that 5 is the correct choice and demands for the Product Owner to proceed to the next story.

In this situation there are a couple of things that are obviously wrong. One, developer α response influenced the estimates of two developers and thus affected the precision of the group estimates. Two, α is certainly adhering to his name and is being too assertive. To maximize the chances of driving precise estimates collaboration should be ensured. Just because a developer is less experienced doesn't mean that they can't contribute something that stimulates the conversation and helps the team gain new insights. Now that we can see how error-prone unstructured group thinking can be, let's look at an example of Planning Poker.

# PLANNING POKER EXAMPLE

**1)** Each developer is given a deck of cards to hold. The numbers will contain a sequence of numbers, the Fibonacci sequence being a popular choice. An example format is as follows: 0, 1/2, 1, 2, 3, 5, 8, 13, 20, 40, 100,?, ∞, ☕. The numbers reflects the developer's opinion of its difficulty, the question mark denotes uncertainty, the infinity symbol denotes that the item is too complex to estimate, and the coffee symbol indicates that a break is needed. The variation in numbers on the cards is irrelevant as what's important is that the team is able to come to an agreement on the complexity of a story while avoiding bias. The Product Owner asks the Dev Team to estimate user-story "Headache" in ideal man-hours.

**2)** The Dev Team individually starts forming mental calculations of how long this will take to implement the story. The Scrum Master goes over the rules to the game and reminds α to not blurt out anything out or less he gets put in the doghouse.

Once the Dev Team has derived their individual estimates they select their card and place it face-down on the table. After everyone has placed down their estimates they're instructed to flip the cards over to reveal the numbers.

**3)** Developer α reports a 5, β reports an 8, ι reports a 13, and ω reports a 40. The Product Owner notices these discrepancies and asks the developers to individually report their reasoning. Developers α and ω were initially in a heated argument but the Scrum Master resolved the issue and made the two shake hands before resuming. Developer α realized that there were some critical components they were over looking and decides to increase their estimate. Developer ω on the other hand saw merits to α logic and realized by using his design that the story would be able to be competed quicker. Developer's β and ι who were initially unconfident on their estimates listened to both sides and feel that they have a higher understanding of the problem. They also did some web-searching and discovered a possible solution they could test. After they have concluded their discussion which only took a couple of minutes, they run another round of estimates.

**4)** Developer α reports a 13, β reports a 20, ι reports a 13, and ω reports 20. SUCCESS. Well, not 100% conformity but the team is in a lot better shape to forming a consensus decision. After discussing a couple of doubts the team decides to give the story a 13. They're ready to tackle the next story.

# FIST OF FIVE (FOF)

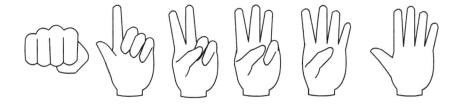

(c) Purcell Media

*Figure 3.2: Fist of Five*

This is a hand-game in which the team forms a consensus non-verbally via hand gestures. It's used in agile teams but has diverse application from trying to get a group of friends to agree on what movie to see, to getting the family to agree on dinner. Below is an illustration of the hand gestures along with their meanings.

Closed fist—I think it's a bad idea and want to block consensus.

1 finger—I have a major issue with it.

2 fingers—I'm not a fan and would like to discuss more.

3 fingers—I'm not entirely in agreement but I'm ok with it passing.

4 fingers—I think it's a good idea.

5 fingers—I think it's a great idea.

## EXAMPLE OF FOF

Scrum Master Adriana calls for the meeting with the Scrum Team "Code Doctors" (CD) on the whim after analyzing some statistics with the Product Owner about the decreased productivity of the team. She time-boxes the event 15-minutes before lunch break via her smart-phone and then kick-starts the conversation.

"According to my research roughly 37% of our bugs are attributed to our legacy system so in order to minimize this occurrence we must come to a consensus on how to re-factor it. A proposed idea will only be implemented if the entire group reports nothing lower than a 4. One idea is to re-design the system as the current one is dated and doesn't enable us to implement new features efficiently. Are you for re-designing the system? Vote in 3...2...1." The developers show their hands high simultaneously—Developer Vadim, an experienced system architect that gave a closed fist to provide his input. He stood up, cleared his throat and then replied.

"If we have unlimited time and budget then perhaps a complete system overhaul can be feasible, albeit difficult. However, the amount of complexity involved in redesigning the architecture will be immense; I imagine 12-months being truly optimistic but more likely we're looking at two years." The rest of the development team chimed in showing their approval for Vadim's response, and Adriana continued.

"OK Team CD, since the majority of the team is against this idea, let's proceed to the next one. Another possible solution to grappling with the legacy code is to implement the "Legacy Code Change Algorithm" that was discussed in the book 'Working Effectively with Legacy Code." Are you for this strategy? Vote in 3...2...1.""

The developers again displayed their gestures simultaneously and Adriana tallied the results. To her satisfaction she sees that three developers gave it a four, while two others gave a five. Everyone around the table get an opportunity to explain their reasoning. Japendra who has been a software engineer for five years and gave it a five was adamant on speaking.

"I have used this method at my last job with positive results. I'm confident that we can apply it to this project to safely re-factor the legacy code without breaking anything." Everyone on the team then had a chance to share their opinion about the matter and Team CD collectively decided to implement the Legacy Code Change Algorithm.

# HOW TO WRITE STELLAR USER-STORIES

In the Stone Age of software development it wasn't uncommon for developers to be handed massive tomes that were called software requirements. Reading through these large documents in a timely manner would be a difficult feat to accomplish. However, with the invention of user-stories gathering requirements can be done in an iterative and incremental manner. This is ideal for software since new technologies and products are constantly being released quickly. It's important for companies to adjust their plans on-the-fly and this is one of the many benefits of user-stories. There are varying definitions of user-stories amongst Agile purists, but my definition is simple.

A **user-story** can be defined as a concise informal description of a requirement from the end-user prospective. User-stories can contain both functional and non-functional requirements and are usually brief enough so that they could be written on an index card or sticky note. The content written on the user-story is important, but the usefulness of it is utilized when thoughtful conversation is invoked. In an ideal situation the buyer and the Scrum Team can get together and collaborate in discovering granular details about the story. It's an adage in software development that customers typically have a difficult time conveying what they want, but they're experts in revealing what they don't want. Both the buyer and the Scrum Team will gain a better understanding of what the customer through thought provoking conversations that will emerge during the creation of the stories. I decided to create a list of the common attributes of user-stories to bring those unfamiliar with the concept up to speed.

## THE TERRIFIC CHECKLIST FOR USER STORIES

Below are some of the typical characteristics of user-stories.

- It comes with acceptance criteria to ensure that the feature has been implemented in accordance to the customer's satisfaction
- It's written from the end-user prospective
- It help developers gain an understanding for the product they are to build
- Answers the 3 W's. **Who** the feature is for, **What** they want, and **Why** they desire it
- Are useful for when the Dev Team are conducting estimates
- Are constructed during the early stages of the project but can be added anytime during its tenure
- Are high-level descriptions and are thus not detailed enough to use for implementation—tasks are added for a more low-level view
- Can link to other documents such as workflows, wireframes, story maps, UML diagrams, etc
- Are typically smaller and contain less technical detail compared to use-cases
- Their simplicity combined with its technology-agnostic format makes it easy for customers to learn
- It should be accessible to everyone involved in the project

## THE THREE C'S

A good way to start invoking the conversation surrounding a story is to use The **Three C's** which stands for Card, Conversation, and Confirmation. Card represents the brevity of user-stories as they should ideally fit on a card, usually the size of 3x5. The typical format for it is: As a <type of user> of the product, I want to <do something>, so that I <benefit>. It's written in the first-person perspective which makes it easy to visualize the end-user. Below is an example of the 3C format.

**As an online instructor**

**I want to create a new course**

**so that I can teach a subject.**

# CARD

By writing user-stories on small index cards you are forced to be concise because it's simply not enough real-estate for being wordy. User-stories are meant to fit inside of a Sprint, and if you have a user-story that's too large then it should be broken down into smaller more manageable chunks and spread across the duration of multiple sprints.

## CONVERSATION

The requirements are elaborated with business people and developers through the conversation in order to gain a better understanding. Think of the card as a placeholder to initiate a conversation—it serves as a topic for a panel discussion and ideally a conversation will follow that helps clarify doubts of the project.

## CONFIRMATION

There should be an agreement between the business owners and developers on the acceptance test for the software in order for them to form a consensus on when a feature is done. This is known as the Definition of Done, and is when an agreement is formed on what it means for the product to be complete.

# INVEST

When writing user-stories a team could apply the INVEST principle so stay grounded off the attributes for a user-story. INVEST is a mnemonic device that stands for Independent, Negotiable, Valuable, Estimable, Small, and Testable. These are all characteristics that describe a well-written story. Below is a description of the component of each phase.

# INDEPENDENT

A user-story should be freed of any dependencies on another story. This is ideal in Scrum since the backlog is continually refined and the order of the backlog items may be shifted throughout the course of the project. If a user-story has any tight-dependencies to other stories then this could make shuffling difficult. Therefore, user-stories should ideally be independent from other stories and self-contained via the INVEST principle.

# NEGOTIABLE

One of the main features of an Agile team is the ability for project requirements to change throughout the course of a project. The product backlog is no exception as items can be edited or removed depending on the conditions throughout its tenure. Even though anyone on the Scrum Team can suggest the addition or subtraction of PBIs, they must negotiate with the Product Owner and get their approval before it's done.

# VALUABLE

The main focus of the user-story is to provide something of value to the end-user. Remember, the software is being made for a certain type of user, and every feature added should represent something that they find useful. There's a saying in business that "The Customer is King" which means that the customers are the ones that ultimately decide what products and services the company produces.

# ESTIMABLE

If a user-story cannot be estimated then it will have difficulties fitting inside the Sprint. Therefore, a story must be polished enough so that developers can estimate the amount of work needed to complete its functionality.

# SMALL

A user-story should be small enough so that it can be completed within the upcoming Sprint. In an ideal scenario, a story should be designed, coded, tested, and integrated within a Sprint—large stories makes this goal unfeasible.

## TESTABLE

The user-story should be testable so that the development team can confirm its accuracy. The more specific the criterion is, the better.

An example of something that's difficult to write a test for is "it should be easy for the instructor to create a course." The generality of the statement makes testing uncertain because there's nothing to explicitly quantify what is "easy." A more refined explanation which removes ambiguity is that "the instructor should be able to create a new course with just two clicks."

# FORMATTING STORIES

If the team decides to write their user-stories on cards then the following is an illustration of a format that they could implement:

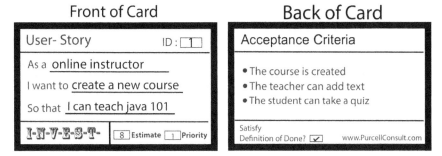

*Figure 3.3: Sample User Story*

Stories are not supposed to be too detailed as the vagueness helps stimulate conversation regarding the domain of what needs to be implemented. Make sure that the stories are written in everyday language to ensure it's written from the end-users perspective.

## WHO SHOULD WRITE USER-STORIES?

One of the values of Agile is customer collaboration over contract negotiation. This snippet of text answers the question of who should write user-stories. Which is ANYONE involved in the project—this can range from customers to developers. User-stories are simple enough so that business people can quickly understand its process and start creating them. However, even though anyone on the team can create user-stories it's the Product Owner who's responsible for prioritizing them in the backlog and therefore has the last say. Order is important as it ensures that the most valuable features are completed first and that dependencies are identified. In an ideal situation this should all be done via collaboration instead of individually. The group conversation will help stimulate cognition and unearth new nuances in the requirements.

## ARE USER-STORIES TECHNICAL?

No. User-stories are high-level descriptions that don't explain much about the technical implementation of the feature. User-stories need to be broken down into **tasks** which are low-level descriptions of the story. This decomposition happens during the Sprint Planning event in which the Dev Team self-organizes to construct the Sprint Backlog and determine how work will be done. The Scrum Guide doesn't list any parameters on the technicality of the Sprint Backlog so my advice is making it as technical as needed. However, it's important to note that the Sprint Planning session is not the only opportunity for the Dev Team to make the user-stories more granular as the team can also do it during Sprint Refinement which is explained in Chapter IV.

## WHAT ARE THE RELATIONSHIPS BETWEEN THEMES, EPICS, STORIES, AND TASKS?

Themes can be defined as the categorization of related user-stories. I.e. a car purchasing app may have themes of car make, model, year, and costs. The respective stories will fall under these themes and can help segment your Scrum Board. Epics are classified as stories that are too large to be completed within an iteration of development. There's no precise quantification for an epic since it varies from team-to-team. However, the general rule of thumb is if your team is having difficulties sizing it, or if the team agrees that it's an extremely complex problem then it's safe to assume that it's an epic not a story. The relationship between epics and user-stories is that several user-stories compose an epic. The relationship between user-stories and tasks are that user-stories are decomposed into tasks which are what developers work on daily. An image that illustrates the relationships between themes, epics, stories, and tasks are listed below:

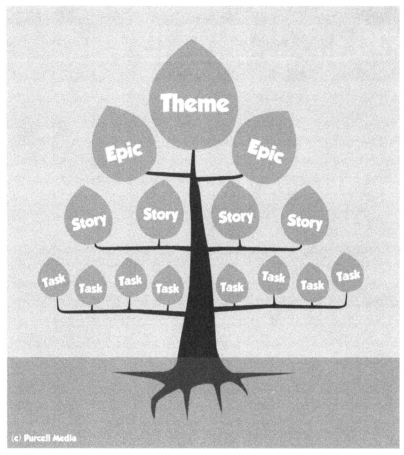

*Figure 3.4: Themes, epics, stories, tasks*

# Chapter III Rewind

In Chapter II we took a high-level tour of the Scrum framework but in this chapter things got more granular. Sprint Planning is the first prescribed event in the Scrum Framework. I refer to this as "Phase I" because all of the activities that take place in this event happen prior to when the Scrum Team gets into actual development. In the Sprint Planning stage the team collaborates, discuss the workload to handle, their goal for the Sprint, and how the work will get done. Once all of these components are figured out the Sprint Backlog is constructed which is the backlog items that the team selects for the upcoming Sprint, the Sprint Goal, and their plan for completing the work. The Sprint Backlog should be made transparent to everyone involved in the project because that's what the team will reference from throughout the tenure of the upcoming Sprint. The Sprint Backlog is not in a static state, as throughout the course of the project it will mutate as more information about the project is collected.

This chapter also discussed several estimation strategies and methods in which teams can form a consensus about a project. In order for teams to give themselves a reasonable chance of obtaining a goal they must be able to reasonably estimate the workload that they can handle. This can be done through practice, in-depth research, and mastering the art of using story points to predict the complexity of stories. A team should know better than to take on more than the amount of workload they can handle in a Sprint, but they should also find that delicate balance of not taking on too little work so that they can satisfy their customers. The Scrum Team must also learn how to use consensus decision making strategies in order to form appropriate decisions quickly. The strategies that were recommended in this chapter were Planning Poker and the Fist of Five.

# Chapter III Sources

1. Mahnic, Viljan. "A Capstone Course on Agile Software Development Using Scrum." doi:10.1109/TE.2011.2142311.

2. Beck, Kent, Mike Beedle, Arie Van Bennekum, Alistair Cockburn, Ward Cunningham, Martin Fowler, James Grenning, Jim Highsmith, Andrew Hunt, Ron Jeffries, Jon Kern, Brian Marick, Robert C. Martin, Steve Mellor, Ken Schwaber, Jeff Sutherland, and Dave Thomas. "Manifesto for Agile Software Development." Manifesto for Agile Software Development. 2001. Accessed August 01, 2016. **http://agilemanifesto.org**.

3. Williams, Wendy M., and Robert J. Sternberg. "Group Intelligence: Why Some Groups Are Better than Others." Science Direct, August 12, 2002. Accessed August 1, 2016. doi:10.1016/0160-2896(88)90002-5.

# Chapter III Quiz

1. **Which of the following is true about the Sprint Backlog?**
   a) Only the Dev Team can modify it
   b) The Dev Team adds items to it
   c) The Dev Team removes items from it
   d) It emerges through the Sprint Plan

2. **Which of the following is true about the Sprint Backlog?**
   a) It belongs solely to the Dev Team
   b) Unnecessary elements of the plan are deleted
   c) The Product Owner can remove or add items
   d) It's highly visible

3. **Select the answer that BEST describes the Sprint Backlog.**
   a) It's the items the entire Scrum team selects for the upcoming Sprint
   b) It's the items that the Dev Team selects for the upcoming Sprint
   c) It's the items that the Dev Team selects for the upcoming Sprint plus the plan for delivering it
   d) It's synonymous to the Product Backlog

4. **Select all that are true regarding the Sprint Backlog.**
   a) It makes the Dev Team's work during the Sprint visible
   b) When work is completed the estimated remaining work is updated
   c) The Sprint Backlog is modified and emerges during the Sprint
   d) It's a real-time view of the work the Dev Team plans to execute

**5.** **True or False: The Sprint Backlog is an intricate plan?**

**6.** **Which of the following are true about the Sprint Goal? Select all that apply.**

    **a)** It's implemented through the backlog

    **b)** It's a Scrum artifact

    **c)** It helps the Dev Team understand why they're building the product

    **d)** It's an output of the Sprint Planning

**7.** **Select all of the following that's true regarding the Sprint Goal**

    **a)** It can be anything

    **b)** It must be approved by the stakeholders

    **c)** The backlog items selected should result in one solid function

    **d)** A possible Sprint Goal could be something that's gets the team to work together

**8.** **Select all of the following that are true regarding the Sprint Goal.**

    **a)** It's an objective set for the Sprint

    **b)** It leaves the Dev Team with no flexibility during the Sprint

    **c)** It's created by the Dev Team ONLY since they're the ones completing the work

    **d)** All of the above

**9.** **True or False: The Sprint Goal is crafted after the Dev Team forecasts what they can complete in the upcoming Sprint.**

**10.** **Select all of the following that are true about Sprint Planning.**

    **a)** The Product Owner makes tradeoffs known to the Dev Team

    **b)** The Dev Team can determine that they have too much work

    **c)** The Dev Team can determine they have too little work

    **d)** The Product Owner helps estimate items in the backlog

**11.** **Select all of the following that are true about Sprint Planning?**

    **a)** Units of work are typically decomposed into units of a day or less

    **b)** No future features are discussed

    **c)** The Product Owner can help demystify backlog items to the Dev Team

    **d)** No negotiating about the selected backlog items should be made

## 12. Select all of the following that are true about Sprint Planning?

    **a)** Enough work is planned for the Dev Team to forecast what they believe they can complete in the upcoming Sprint

    **b)** The first couple of days of work are planned

    **c)** Work could be of varying size and effort

    **d)** The plan the Scrum Team creates is static

## 13. Select all of the following that are true about Sprint Planning?

    **a)** What can be delivered in the upcoming Sprint is answered.

    **b)** Whose working on what is answered.

    **c)** How the Dev Team will self-organize is answered.

    **d)** All of the above

Choice (d) is correct. Refer to page 9 of The Scrum Guide for further details.

## 14. Which of the following are true about Sprint Planning? Select all that apply.

    **a)** The Product Owner only creates the Sprint Goal

    **b)** The entire Scrum Team collaborates to understand the work of the Sprint

    **c)** Stakeholders attend to answer any concerns for the Scrum Team

    **d)** The Dev Team ONLY decides how many items they complete for the upcoming Sprint

## 15. What's the maximum amount of time allocated for Sprint Planning?

    **a)** 2 hours

    **b)** 4 hours

    **c)** 8 hours

    **d)** None of the above

## 16. Which of the following are true about Sprint Planning? Select all that apply.

    **a)** The Dev Team forecasts what will be completed during the upcoming Sprint

**b)** The Scrum Master makes sure the Scrum Team understand the purpose of it

**c)** The Product Owner states objectives of the Sprint Goal

**d)** Choices a and c only

### 17. Select all that are true about Sprint Planning.

**a)** By the end the Dev Team should tell the Product Owner and Scrum Master how they'll self -organize

**b)** Unit tests are created for the user-stories with the highest order

**c)** The Dev Team may collaborate with those OUTSIDE the Scrum Team for technical advice

**d)** The Dev Team has a Daily Scrum and discusses the Sprint Backlog

### 18. True or False: the inputs into the Sprint Planning event are: product backlog, latest product increment, projected capacity of the Dev Team, and past performance of the Dev Team.

### 19. Select the BEST answer regarding the Deliveries of a "Done" product.

**a)** Ensuring that the entire product is DONE

**b)** Ensuring that there's always a potentially useful version of the product available

**c)** They're always released by the end of the development cycle

**d)** All of the above

### 20. Which of the following about the definition of "Done" (DoD) is correct?

**a)** Everyone on the team must understand it

**b)** This definition varies SIGNIFICANTLY by Scrum Team

**c)** It's used to access when the Scrum Team is finished planning

**d)** When Scrum Team members have a shared understanding of DONE this elucidates transparency

### 21. Which of the following about the definition of "Done" (DoD) is correct?

**a)** If it's part of the organizational guidelines all the Scrum Teams must follow it

**b)** It helps the Scrum Team select the quantity of PBIs for the upcoming Sprint

**c)** Different Scrum Teams can have their own DoD

**d)** All of the above

22. **Which of the following about the definition of "Done" (DoD) is correct?**

**a)** Once defined the DoD doesn't change

**b)** Each product should have a standard DoD

**c)** The DoD is only applicable to the final Increment in the Sprint

**d)** The DoD is more about meeting stakeholders' expectations than technical ones

23. **True or False: The Definition of DONE implies that the Increment MUST be in a useable condition AND it must adhere to the Scrum Team's definition of DONE.**

24. **True or False: Writing a unit test for each user-story is a valid DoD.**

# Chapter III Quiz Answers

1. Choices (a), (b), and (c) are correct. Choice (d) is incorrect because it emerges through the Sprint.

2. Choices (a), (b), and (d) are correct. Choice (c) is incorrect because this privilege is reserved for the Dev Team.

3. Choice (c) only. This is the definition in accordance to the Scrum Guide. Read the section about the Sprint Backlog in Chapter III for additional details.

4. All of the above is true.

5. False, it's a plan with just enough detail. It should be detailed enough so that the Dev Team understands their work but it should not be overly detailed as doing so makes change difficult.

6. Choices (a), (c), and (d) is correct. The Sprint Goal is not an artifact; it's the objective that's constructed during Sprint Planning to help the Scrum Team stay on track during the Sprint.

7. Choices (c) and (d) are correct. Sprint Goal should be relevant to the goals of the company and The Scrum Team decides it.

8. Choice (a) only. The Sprint Goal gives the Dev Team some flexibility, and it's created by The Scrum Team as a whole.

9. True. According to the Scrum Guide the Sprint Goal is crafted after the Dev Team forecasts the backlog items they can complete in the upcoming Sprint.

10. Choices (a), (b), and (c) are correct. Choice (d) is incorrect because The Dev Team is responsible for estimating the backlog items

11. Choices (a) and (c) are correct. The reason choice (b) is not correct is because while long term plans are not considered part of the criteria of Agile, it's not a bad idea to talk about future features that could tie in directly to what is being done. Choice (d) is incorrect as negotiating is allowed.

12. Choices (a), (b), and (c) are correct. The Scrum Guide never mentions that the Sprint Plan is static so it has a possibility as long it's not so extreme it deviate from the Sprint Goal. However, before the plan is changed the Dev Team should consult with the Product Owner for transparency.

13. Choice (d) is correct. Refer to the section about Sprint Planning in Chapter III for additional details.

14. Choices (b) and (d) are correct. The Scrum Team as a whole creates the Sprint Goal. The stakeholders wouldn't need to attend as that's what the Sprint Review is for.

15. Choice (c) is correct. A 4-week Sprint is allocated a maximum of 8 hours for planning the upcoming Sprint.

16. Choices (a), (b), and (c) are correct. Refer to the section about the Sprint Goal for further clarification.

17. Choices (a) and (c) are correct. Choices (b) and (d) are incorrect as they happen once the team starts building the product Increment.

18. True. Refer to the Sprint Goal section for additional clarification.

19. Choice (b) only. Multiple deliveries of definition of done ensures that there's always a working version of the product available for release.

20. Choices (a) (b) and (d) are all correct. Choice (c) is incorrect because it's used to access when The Scrum Team have completed a product increment.

21. Choices (a) and (b) are correct. Choice (c) is incorrect because all Scrum Teams must mutually agree to a coherent DoD.

22. Choice (b) is correct. Choice (a) is incorrect because it does change as more information about the product is gathered. Choice (c) is incorrect because a DoD could be applied to other instances of the Sprint, such as the user-stories. Choice (d) is incorrect because the DoD serves more as a quality assurance check for the technical specs of the project.

23. True. It's important that the Increment meets these requirements so that the Product Owner can decide to release it if they desire to.

24. True. It's ultimately up to the team to decide, and if they agree that it is beneficial to producing a quality product then it can be included.

# CHAPTER IV:

# Execution Phase

In the previous section you learned about Sprint Planning which helps prepare the team for the Sprint. This chapter covers everything that takes place during the development phase of the Sprint. This is where the Dev Team will spend the bulk of their time at. The typical day of a Scrum Team is kick-started with the Daily Scrum which is a daily meeting that occurs during the Sprint. The Dev Team self-organizes and updates each other of their progress. Once that is done the team exit the meeting and then go onto start building the code. This process happens repeatedly until the closure of the Sprint. If everything goes according to plan then at the end of the Sprint the team will be left with a shippable product Increment. Let's start learning about the Sprint by studying the central event in this component which is the Daily Scrum.

# Example of a Daily Scrum Meeting

The Daily Scrum is a somewhat infamous occurrence in Scrum. In this event the team meets daily typically before they start developing to discuss their status along with any potential impediments that are prohibiting their advancement. The team is allocated a maximum of fifteen minutes for the Daily Scrum, regardless of the length of the Sprint. Here's a hypothetical scenario of an effectively ran daily standup. The developers arrive to work early in order to mitigate traffic congestions, converse with each other, and brew some fresh coffee. While they're enjoying their coffee-chat the timer suddenly rings and the familiar melody from *O Fortuna* starts to play. That's a cue for the Dev Team to congregate next to the large whiteboard and discuss the three questions which are:

1. What have I accomplished yesterday?
2. What will I accomplish today?
3. What are the impediments blocking my progress?

The team learned the rules of the standup from the Scrum Master and they self-organized to figure out which format works best for them. They have a policy in which they rotate who kick-starts the discussion. After one developer is finished answering the three questions they pass a squish-ball to who they want to speak next. While the team is having a thought provoking discussion the timer once again goes off with the *Merrie Melodies Closing Theme*—this cues the developers to promptly end the discussion. Developers that would like to elaborate on technical problems do so outside of the standup meeting.  This is one example of how a Scrum Team may decide to conduct a standup but there are many variations that a team can decide to implement. A team new to Scrum could think that daily stand-ups are a silly nuisance that should be avoided—

they make think its needless drivel and that their time would be better invested doing coding. However, it's the Scrum Master's job to convince the team about the benefits of the standup and to coach them on how to correctly implement it. The following section highlights the dos' and don'ts of the meeting.

# THE DOS AND DON'TS OF STAND-UPS

**DO MASTER THE RULES:** The Scrum Master is the "keeper of Scrum" and they should know all of the rules of it and then transfer this knowledge to the Dev Team. One of the concepts that I like to reinforce daily into the Dev Team's psyche is that all 3 questions should be answered within the allocated 15-minute time-box. If the Dev Team is struggling with correctly applying the standup then the Scrum Master can decide to host a workshop and coach the team through a simulation.

**DO MONITOR SPRINT GOAL AND PROGRESS:** One of the key benefits to running the standup is that the Dev Team will actively monitor the status of the project. One of the three questions that are asked is, "are there any impediments that's blocking your progress?" This question will help identify any roadblocks that the developers are facing such as build failures for example. Once the impediments are discovered the team can self-organize and resolve the issues after the standup. The team could monitor the project progress through updating the burn down charts by summing up all of the outstanding work. By consistently analyzing this data they should gain a better understanding of if they're close or far from obtaining their Sprint Goal.

**DO HAVE A GOOD TIME:** Most people don't look forward to meetings for various reasons such as lack of engagement, information overload, and unclear agenda. However, there are no rules that prohibit a daily standup from being fun and engaging. In the "Daily Scrum FAQs" section I provide tips on how a team can spice up their stand-ups.

**DON'T DISCUSS TECHNICAL DETAILS:** Believe it or not these types of discussions should be avoided at all costs during the standup. The reason being is difficult technical issues could take a while to resolve and should thus be discussed after the conclusion of the standup. Having elaborate technical discussions will more than likely disrupt the rhythm of the standup and cause the team to surpass the fifteen minute time-box. Therefore, apply the KISS principle to the standup and leave the technical discussions out.

**DON'T MICROMANAGE:** The daily standup is for developers, by developers. The purpose is not to put the Dev Team under the microscope of management but to instead serve as a constant point of communication throughout the duration of the project. It's not a status reporting meeting, it's a team meeting.

The Dev Team doesn't report the 3 questions to the Scrum Master but instead report it to the entire Dev Team—they're the ones who are responsible for conducting the meeting while the Scrum Master ensures that they're doing it correctly. The Dev Team is the only team members that should be present during the standup—if there's any information that the Product Owner, Scrum Master, or stakeholders should be aware of the then this information should be radiated through whatever means the team chooses. For example, they may radiate key information by posting sticky notes on a whiteboard, highlighting text in Google Docs, or setting up a wallboard in Jira.

**DON'T VARY LOCATION/TIME:** The only restriction for the location is that it's in an open space large enough to comfortably fit the team in a circular format, similar to a football huddle. It would be inconvenient to hold the meeting in a space that could obstruct the flow of foot traffic so keep that in mind. I wouldn't suggest holding the stand-ups in the basement or rooftop of the building as that's just hmm... different—a popular choice is near the whiteboard. Once the team agrees on the spot to host the standup they should stick to that location like glue. It's important that the schedule of the stand-ups is consistent daily. If the team is constantly waiting on one developer that's habitually late then they need to be reminded in a professional manner that their timely presence is important to the success of the stand-up. The only way they should be excused from arriving late is if they bring in a box full of freshly made bagels for the entire team. In the next section I'm going to list some commonly asked questions regarding the daily standup. The purpose of this is to serve as a set of heuristics that the Scrum Team can refer to whenever they run into issues regarding the standup.

# DAILY SCRUM FAQS
## Q: CAN DISTRIBUTED TEAMS CONDUCT A DAILY STANDUP?

Yes, it's increasingly common. There are endless technology options that allow developers scattered across the globe to apply a digital version of the standup to their daily routine—some examples include email, instant messaging, intranet discussion forums, video chat, videoconferencing, or other communication platforms. Each technology inherently presents their own unique pros and cons so it's up to the team to analyze them and select a solution that's suitable for their company. Whatever technology the team decides to use I would recommend that there is first an information sharing session on how to use it. If only two out of five developers know how to use the new teleconferencing software the team recently purchased, then this will present delays in the Daily Scrum. A research study backs up this assertion as it states it's the newness of the technology NOT the team that leads to poor communication in computer groups. [1]

However, the technology familiarity is just one obstacle that the distributed team will encounter. Another one is how does company XYZ get past the fact that two developers are located in San Francisco, one in Auckland New Zealand, one in Bengaluru India, one in Yekateninburg Russia, and yet another in Chongqing China? One solution is to try and find a time that is doable, not ideal, for everyone on the team. An ideal time probably doesn't exist, but the point I like to stress is that the daily standup is only fifteen minutes so if everyone can find the sweet-spot in which there is enough downtime to squeeze in the standup then that would be beneficial to the entire team. I would recommend that everyone gets familiar with each other's time zone instead of guessing what time it is for their colleagues. One simple method that I recommend is what I call the "virtual glue." Every developer part of a virtual team should create and share their daily schedule through a means the team agrees upon, such as Google Calendar.

How granular each developer gets is up to them but at a minimum they should place: their time zone, the time blocks they work, their lunch breaks, and when they're unavailable. To build familiarity with different time zones use the World Clock: http://www.timeanddate.com/worldclock.

## Q: DOES THE TEAM HAVE TO MEET FACE-TO-FACE? CAN WE USE E-MAIL, IM, VIDEO CHAT, OR SOME OTHER FORM OF TECHNOLOGY?

If the team is collocated then I would recommend using face-to-face (FTF) communication as the primary method of communication. This doesn't mean that other methods are not useful as many of them are— The open source format for example is a testament that distributed teams can collaborate to produce high-quality software. However, this doesn't mean that the methods used for developing open source software are better than those for developing closed-source ones. A study confirmed that there's no conclusive evidence that shows that one has a dominate quality advantage over the other. [2]

There are two case studies that I would recommend reading to analyze the benefits of FTF communication compared to computer mediated communication (CMC). The first compares FTF to teleconferences and electronic chat. The conclusion was that CMC methods tend to generate more ideas and produce a higher cognitive load leading to poorer comprehension. [3] Another study compared groups using FTF to CMC and concluded that compared to FTF it performed poorly for selecting proposed solutions. [4]

If the Dev Team is adamant on using a CMC in their daily standup then they have the right to experiment par the daily standup. However, it needs to be benchmarked against FTF in order to determine which method was more beneficial to the team.

## Q: WHAT HAPPENS IF A DEVELOPER IS ABSENT FROM THE DAILY SCRUM?

It's possible for a developer to be absent due to illness, vacation, or anything unexpected. This is an issue that most companies will face sooner or later, not just Scrum Teams. I prefer to group the types of absences into two categories which are expected and unexpected— expected denotes something that the team is aware of before the Sprint starts and unexpected ones happen without any foresights during a Sprint. If the team were aware that "Developer Joe" have been planning his dream vacation to "Bora Bora" for months then they have time to self-organize and devise a plan on how to distribute Joe's workload across the team prior to his departure. It's important for the team to acknowledge Joe's contribution during Sprint Planning. For example, if Joe works predominately on a specialized part of the system then it would be logical for the team to reduce their workload unless Joe proactively cross-pollinated his knowledge to them.

When an employee is unexpectedly absent I would recommend for the Scrum Master to host an impromptu meeting with the team to revise the Sprint Goal. The Product Owner should classify the importance of completing the Sprint within the current cycle. If it's something that's critical like the final Sprint before the product is shipped then that's a deadline that the company doesn't want to miss. The Dev Team can analyze the stories the developer was responsible for and distribute their workload evenly so that no developer is carrying the bulk of the additional work. In this situation communication becomes even more critical, and if it's the first time the team is in a predicament like this then they'll quickly discover how cross-functional they really are. Ideally, the Scrum Team has been consistently sharing information in company wikis, forums, blogs, docs, etc so that they can reference it in timely situations like this. This is an unattractive situation because regardless of the even distribution of workload, each developer's workload will temporary be increased which is not ideal. This can be mitigated by the Product Owner who can negotiate with both the Dev Team and the key stakeholders to re-prioritize the backlog so that both parties are satisfied. I don't recommend for the Scrum Team to bring on additional developers in a situation like this. A popular software engineering adage is found in the popular book "The Mythical Man-Month" by Fredrick Brook—it states that "adding additional resources to a project makes it later."

## Q: SPRINT ITEM TAKES LONGER THAN EXPECTED. WHAT SHOULD WE DO?

Don't panic! This is not uncommon in the early stages of the project in which the team is still ironing on the kinks in their process. If the team discovers that they have a few incomplete stories left at the end of the Sprint then they need to inspect why this is the case and adapt a new plan to eradicate this from resurfacing. Having incomplete stories at the end of a Sprint doesn't bode well with management which is why the team should habitually monitor their progress during the Daily Scrum—prevention is key in this context. If the team knows in advance that they bit off more than they can chew then this is easier to mitigate than notices last minute before the deadline. It's important for the team to understand that they should 1) deliver what they agree to and 2) deliver working software at the end of the Sprint. It's a problem if the team is nowhere close to delivering what they agreed to at the end of a Sprint. A possible cause for this is poor requirements management from either the customer, Scrum Team, or both. If the customer is continually making additional requests during the Sprint then tradeoffs needs to be made as the Scrum Team have already forecasted the workload they can handle. Refer back to Chapter III and read the section for Estimation Strategies if your team needs more education on this topic.

## Q: WE USUALLY COMPLETE THE DAILY STANDUP IN 5-MINUTES. IS THIS OK?

No. The purpose of the standup is 1) for the team to inspect and adapt their process and 2) to monitor the status of the project. The common ways to doing this is for every developer to answer the three questions of what you did yesterday, what you will do today, and are there any impediments in your way? I think it's fair to say that in this busy world people are struggling to remember simple things like what they ate for dinner yesterday, so trying to recall what they did yesterday takes some cognition. The next question of "what you will be doing today" shouldn't be too brief or less the person is not planning on doing much. Lastly, knowing what's causing delays in progress is not something that's simple to communicate succinctly. Therefore, my conclusion is five minutes for the daily standup may be suitable for a "team" of two developers, otherwise plan on utilizing the full fifteen minutes. Most Dev Teams usually have a problem with exceeding the fifteen minute mark which can be resolved by continual information sharing from the Scrum Master to the Dev Team. Daily reminders like staying focused on the 3 questions, saying more with less, and reserving the technical discussions until afterwards are some simple remedies.

## Q: STAND-UPS ARE BORING. ARE THERE WAYS TO SPICE THEM UP?

Of course! I'm an advocate of making them both fun and informative. My advice is for the Scrum Master to ask each developer to jot down one fun activity that they would like to implement during the standup. The ideas can then be pooled and the team can collectively vote on the activities. If there are any overlaps then that's great, but there's a high probability that there won't be so the team can collectively decide how they determine the winners. Obviously it's recommended for these ideas to be succinct so that it doesn't extend the meeting past the 15-minute time-box. Some strategies I recommend for adding spice to stand-ups are coffee or tea, food, music, comedy, silly objects, and a pinch of salt... well ignore the last option.

If the company doesn't have a spare coffee maker then someone could donate or purchase one for the team. I'm not a coffee connoisseur but

I would recommend investing in a bean grinder and grinding beans onsite vs. purchasing grinded beans for a fresher Cup of Joe—if the team prefers tea then investing in a tea maker would be the route to take. Food is something that tends to get people excited and the team can designate a day during the week like hump day for example for a team breakfast—items like bagels, donuts, or pastries are common—the team could rotate who brings in breakfast weekly. Energizing music could get the team in the mood for the meeting—the team can discuss which theme songs will prompt the beginning and end of the meeting. Mirthful laughter is something that's nice to hear among a team, and displaying a funny meme or looping a YouTube comedy may do the trick. Last but not least the team can pass objects to indicate who gets to speak next. It can be something silly like a slinky, an emoji face squeeze ball, or even a Frisbee, but as long the team gets a thrill out of passing it then it has done its job.

# Monitoring Progress

In order for a team to apply the concepts of Scrum they must be able to monitor progress. Once the plan is finalized and the team gets into the development phase, discerning eyes must be placed on the process. If the team is continually running into bottlenecks then it's clear that something needs to change, but what exactly? The team must refine their methods of monitoring the project status and be able to quickly resolve problems that arise. If a team quickly makes changes, but it's the wrong one, then that negates the benefit of Agile and creates a cluster of problems. In this section you'll discover prescribed methods for actively monitoring the progress of the project along with recommendations on how to improve the process.

## SCRUM THEORY

Scrum utilizes empirical process theory or *empiricism* in order to continually improve the software development process. The premise of this theory is that all knowledge comes from sense or experience. This theory gave rise to experimental sciences which relies on designing, executing, and interpreting scientific experiments. According to historians, Thales of Miletus is considered the first scientist. He was a pre-Socratic Greek philosopher that conducted many experiments in order to learn more about the world around him. Experimentation and learning from those results is such an important concept in sciences that you can see elements in all of them. For example, some groundbreaking works that have been discovered due to scientists experimenting are Albert Einstein's mass-energy equivalence which is the famous equation of $E = mc^2$. The world is a more interesting place due to scientists that have conducted experiments and discovered new concepts. A Scrum Team that continually inspects and adapts have a better chance of producing quality software

There are three pillars to Scrum Theory: transparency, inspection, and adaptation. **Transparency** describes a state in which an object is easy to be seen. Transparency is beneficial in a team environment as it helps elucidate communication. The Scrum Guide states that components of the team process must be visible to those who are responsible for the outcome. It also provides two examples of it which are 1) a common language regarding the process must be shared with the team and 2) the Scrum Team and the project sponsors must have a common Definition of Done. [6]

Another way that I like to describe transparency is as the unambiguous communication and comprehension between a team. When a group of people read a poem there will be several different interpretations of it. When a team discuss a technical problem it's possible for communication and interpretation to become fragmented. Therefore, it's recommended for the Scrum Team to understand each other to the T. When communication breakdowns arise in a team then disorder is bound to happen.

**Inspection** is the process in which artifacts are carefully analyzed to ensure that it's adhering to the standards of the team. Since artifacts are radiated to everyone involved the inspection can be done in a non-intrusive manner in order to not disrupt the progress of the Dev Team. Remember, Scrum is against strict management so developers shouldn't report what they have been working on to management daily. Instead, the Dev Team self-organize and report their progress in the daily stand-ups which can be tracked via burn down charts.

**Adaption** is the process in which changes are assimilated into the team. We all know how to inspect our diet for example. Simply cut out excess sugars, fats, and processed carbohydrates and eat a clean well-balanced diet coupled with daily exercise. However, making the adaptation into your life is quite difficult, especially if there's a habit of making unhealthy choices. Therefore, a plan must be devised in order for adaptation to manifest or else its simply wishful thinking. When the Dev Team is aware that there's something troubling in the process then they can discuss these details during any of the prescribed events in Scrum. Since the Daily Scrum is an event that happens daily within the Sprint it's a key opportunity for the team to inspect and adapt their process. There's a prescribed event at the very end of the Sprint known as the Sprint Retrospective. This is a formal opportunity for the Scrum Team to inspect, adapt, and create a plan for implementing those changes in the next Sprint. This is discussed in detail in Chapter V.

# THE LOW DOWN ON THE BURN DOWN

The burn down chart is the most common method used by Scrum Teams to display important data that relates to the progress of the project. As the name suggests, these charts illustrate the rate in which the team is *burning* through their customer's user-stories. Its main metric known as velocity is computed by summing up the amount of stories a team completes per Sprint. These simple yet powerful graphs can convey an array of helpful information to Scrum Teams and help assist them greatly with making critical decisions for their project. It's time to feel the burn and learn more about these charts.

## BURN DOWN CHARTS BENEFITS

**HELP THE TEAM PAINT A REALISTIC PICTURE:** When a Scrum Team first starts a project they are most likely affected by *optimism quagmire*. This is a common occurrence amongst inexperienced teams in which they believe they can complete a project in an unrealistic short timeframe. As the developers start to get deep amidst the project reality settles in and they realize that they bit off more than they can chew. The good news is burn down charts will help reveal the team's velocity which shows how many stories they're moving per Sprint. The team will need to get a couple of development iterations under their belt in order to gain a more accurate picture of their velocity as this metric will likely have a high variability within the first couple of Sprints. When the team has irrefutable data with their past performance this can help assist them with making future decisions in the project.

**DISPLAYS THE EFFECTS OF THE DECISIONS:** One can argue that we're at our respective points in life by an accumulation of the decisions we made—I like to apply this concept to projects. Some of the decisions a Scrum Team made may display good insight while others may not. The difficulty with decision making is that it's impossible for the team to have the intuition to ALWAYS make the correct decision. Therefore, it's helpful for the team to dig into their past and analyze which decisions were appropriate or not. The burn down chart can help radiate this information to the Scrum Team. It can also help them team in making future decisions.

**HELP THE TEAM IN FUTURE DECISION MAKING:** One of the most important metrics of these tools is that the team has concrete data of what they successfully accomplished in the past which can aid in future decision making. For example, if a team averaged 4 story points the last five Sprints then it will most likely be a poor decision to try and aim for 8 story points the next one. Five or six story points may not be unreasonable if the team gelled with each other, gained a strong understanding of the system, and have a realistic picture of the appropriate workload they can handle—however, going outside the scope of the team's capability without no data to support it is a risky venture.

**VERSATILE TOOLS:** Even though they're typically used in Scrum and Agile based products, burn down chart can in theory be used for many projects in which an individual or team wants to measure the rate they complete work. The team needs to devise a plan and then transpose it to a burn down chart. The easiest way to doing this is to figure out the units of time and work that they'll use. The time-unit should be reflective on the size of a project. For example constructing a skyscraper can take many months, but writing a college essay can be done in hours so think about it carefully before committing. Once the appropriate unit is selected the next step is to determine the units for work. Remember, story points are an arbitrary unit used to predict the difficulty of user-stories but if a project is small in scope then using tasks as a unit of work may be the better option. Once the units of work are decomposed into more granular modules and estimated the burn down chart can be constructed. However, building the burn down chart is just the beginning as the real power is when insights are derived from the data.

# CRASH COURSE TO BURN-DOWN CHARTS

Let's get a deeper understanding about burn down charts by looking at some examples. Let's look at a typical burn down chart in an ideal situation indicated below.

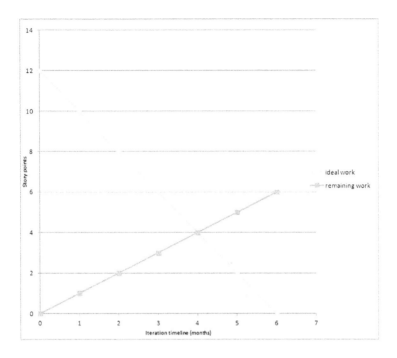

*Figure 4.1: Idealistic Sprint scenario*

A Scrum team can frequently refer to these charts to get a rough idea of how much work they have remaining. For example, according to figure 4.1 the team initially predicted that their workload would be 12-story points which are what the chart is initially set to.

By the end of month one the team has successfully completed two story points so the total work remaining is now 10—after month two the team has completed another two story points so the initial work remaining is now 8—the team is cruising along at a steady velocity of two story points per Sprint and by month 6 the team has completed a total of 12 story points.

While the team was working on the project they could view their progress by looking at the amount of points they were completing per month. If the team was deviating significantly from their plan then they need to inspect and adapt their process and identify what's causing the delay.

Now, let's take a look at another chart that reflects a more realistic scenario.

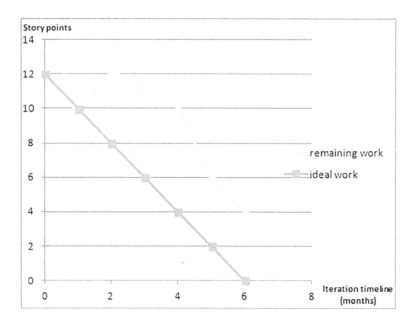

*Figure 4.2: Realistic Sprint Scenario*

Figure 4.1 is hyper-unrealistic because teams don't predictably complete work in such a linear state. In the beginning phase there's a learning process that they go through which will result in temporary deviations. Figure 4.2 is a more accurate example of a typical burn down chart. Let's learn how to interpret it. The X-axis represents time and common variables used to depict this are hours, days, weeks, and months. The Y-axis represents work which is usually depicted by tasks or points. Figure 4.2 uses months to represent time and points to represent work.

**The project starting point** is the point that's located farthest to the left on the graph while the **project ending point** is the point that's located farthest to the right and signals the completion of the project. In the above figure the starting point is at Month 0 and the ending point is at Month 6. The **Ideal work remaining** is a linear line on a burn down chart that depicts the summations of all of the estimates. It begins at the starting point which depicts the estimated amount of stories for the Sprint and ends at the ending point which indicates the completion of the stories. In the above figure the team's ideal scenario is to complete two story points per Sprint. The ideal work remaining is very telling about the progress the team is making. If the actual work completed is above the line then that tells the team that they're running behind schedule. On the contrary if the actual work done is below the ideal work time then that tells the team that they're ahead of schedule.

The **actual work remaining** shows how much work the team is completing per Sprint. In the above figure you can see that the team initially completes two story points so after the first Sprint they have 10 story points left. However, after the second Sprint they have 12 story points left! This is not an uncommon situation in software projects and can happen because the development team underestimated the workload of a story, or that the customer is requesting additional features. However, after the second Sprint the team starts to gel and is making better progress. The team doesn't quite meet their goal by Month 6 as they're four story points short but by looking at the data it's apparent that they have gained a better understanding of the product as time progressed. In order to **compute the velocity** from the graph, you must sum up all of work the team has done within the Sprints. In this example 10 story points were completed over the course of six Sprints so that's the velocity. In order to get the average velocity of the release just divide the total number of story points by the total number of Sprints which equates to roughly 1.67 story points per Sprint—this is a .33 point differential between the goal of two story points. It's important to analyze the Sprints in which impediments arise and discover why it happened and how to prevent it from occurring in the future.

# TO BE, OR NOT TO BE — CANCELING A SPRINT

A Sprint can be canceled under extreme circumstances like if the Sprint Goal is no longer applicable to the team. According to the Scrum Guide the responsibility of canceling a Sprint is given to the Product Owner, but in reality the whole team has a role in it. For example, if the Dev Team did a poor job estimating user-stories and discovers that their one-week Sprint will take eight weeks then the Product Owner will most likely cancel after consulting the Scrum Team and stakeholders.

The Product Owner should monitor internal and external conditions to see what's happening that can potentially affect the health of the Sprint. An internal factor could be if the company decides to shift in a different direction while the Sprint is in progress. Let's say that a software company that made its riches selling retail boxed software decided amongst its C-suite executives that they must discontinue these operations and shift to a cloud based solution. The Product Owner who's in contact with the stakeholders realizes that their decision will ultimately make the Sprint Goal pointless so decides to cancel it. The good news is Sprint cancelations are atypical due to their short duration. All options should be intensely studied before reaching the final verdict. Imagine that you're a developer that has just solved a difficult problem that took days to complete only to find out that it's not useable due to the Sprint getting canceled. That's a pretty dramatic example but I think you get the point.

# Backlog Refinement

**Product backlog refinement** or backlog grooming is the continual process in which the Product Owner in conjunction with the Dev Team adds specifications, estimates, and order to the backlog items. The Scrum Team is responsible for determining how and when this is done and the entire process shouldn't consume more than 10% of the Dev Team's capacity.

The input into the backlog refinement session is the product backlog items while the output will be more granular product backlog items. Since the Scrum Master is the guardian of Scrum knowledge I would recommend that they study, research, and experiment with solid principles for conducting a beneficial session. Reinforcing that the team time-box the session to maximize efficiency, collaborate on refinement to increase shared understanding, and that it's continually held are some of the key principles I recommend. Even though the Scrum Guide recommends that the team collaborates to determine the optimal time and format for the refinement session there are a couple of strategies I recommend. Most Scrum Teams hold their refinement session amidst a Sprint, such as a couple of days before the end of it. Once the Sprint is coming to a closure the developers can start thinking about refining the stories for the next Sprint.

This preparation will help make the upcoming Sprint Planning session flow smoothly; otherwise planning and extensive refinement will be done within Sprint Planning which can be arduous. If the refinement session is held towards the end of a Sprint then the Dev Team has real-world application of attacking the problems and will thus be in a better position to provide more accurate data. The Product Owner can therefore generate a backlog that is less ambiguous and better prioritized. In an ideal situation everyone from the Dev Team will attend the refinement session but realistically this may not be feasible depending on the intensity of the current Sprint. The team must agree on a strategy on how to share the information with those who can't attend. The Product Owner should take this as the perfect opportunity to add clarity to the backlog. I would recommend partitioning the stories that will occur in subsequent Sprints into three main modules: ready, soon, and later. Ready will denote the stories that are refined to the tee and are instantly eligible for inclusion in the upcoming Sprint Backlog. "Soon" indicates stories that are of high importance but it still need more decomposition before it could be useful to the Dev Team. "Later" indicates stories that still has a cloud of ambiguity around it and needs a lot of work done before it can be useful to the Dev Team.

# Chapter IV Rewind

In this chapter you learned about the components that consist of the Sprint. The chapter started off with an example of a Daily Scrummeeting—the standup is an event that occurs daily during the duration of the Sprint and is a critical time for the Dev Team to communicate with each other. They are to report their progress, state what they'll accomplish that day, and indentify any impediments that are hindering their progress. It's important that the standup is time-boxed to fifteen minutes so that the team doesn't waste precious resources which the Scrum Master coaches them on. In addition, methods in which a team can monitor their progress were introduced. Delivering high-quality software by project deadlines should be a main priority of the Dev Team throughout the Sprint. A common method for tracking progress in Scrum Teams is burn down charts which displays work vs. time. The burn down chart should be updated frequently throughout the course of the project and by actively monitoring it will help Scrum Teams predict if they'll finish the project on schedule.

# Chapter IV Resources

1. Hollingshead, Andrea B., Joseph E. Mcgrath, and Kathleen M. O'Connor. "Group Task Performance and Communication Technology A Longitudinal Study of Computer-Mediated Versus Face-to-Face Work Groups." Accessed August 1, 2016. doi:10.1177/1046496493243003.

2. Raghunathan, Srinivasan, Ashutosh Prasad, Birendra K. Mishra, and Hsihui Chang. Open Source versus Closed Source: Software Quality in Monopoly and Competitive Markets. October/November 2005. Accessed August 1, 2016. http://ai.ia.agh.edu.pl/wiki/_media/pl:miw:2009:2005_raghunathan_-_open_source_versus_closed_source.pdf.

3. Bordia, Prashant. "Face-to-Face Versus Computer-Mediated Communication: A Synthesis of the Experimental Literature." International Journal of Business Communication. Accessed August 1, 2016. doi:10.1177/002194369703400106.

4. Daly, Bonita L. "The Influence of Face-to-face versus Computer-mediated Communication Channels on Collective Induction." Science Direct, May 12, 2002. Accessed August 1, 2016. doi:10.1016/0959-8022(93)90006-R.

5. Brooks, Frederick P. The Mythical Man-month: Essays on Software Engineering.

6. Schwaber, Ken, and Jeff Sutherland. The Scrum Guide. July/August 2016. Accessed August 1, 2016. http://www.scrumguides.org/docs/scrumguide/v2016/2016-Scrum-Guide-US.pdf.

# Chapter IV Quiz

**1. Select all that are true about the Sprint.**

    **a)** It's time-boxed

    **b)** It's the container for ALL prescribed events

    **c)** It's recommended to keep them consistent

    **d)** They restart once the next daily Scrum starts

**2. Select all that are true about the Sprint.**

    **a)** It can't be canceled

    **b)** It's considered the "heart" of Scrum

    **c)** It MUST create a product increment at the end of the cycle

    **d)** The development is done before it starts

**3. Select all that are true about the Sprint.**

    **a)** Development work is part of the Sprint

    **b)** Quality goals cannot be minimized

    **c)** No negotiation about the scope is permitted

    **d)** No changes are allowed

**4. Select all that are true about the Sprint.**

    **a)** It's a project with a 1-month maximum time-limit

    **b)** They have an associated goal

    **c)** Under special circumstances a Sprint can exceed a month

    **d)** They minimize risk due to short cycles

5. **Which of the following are valid arguments for the short timeframe of a Sprint? Select all that apply.**

   **a)** Reduces odds of fluctuating requirements

   **b)** Minimizes chances of complexity increasing

   **c)** Minimizes chances for risk

   **d)** Choices (a) and (c) only

6. **Can a Sprint be canceled? If so, select all that apply.**

   **a)** It's not possible

   **b)** DONE backlog items are reviewed

   **c)** Incomplete backlog items are re-estimated

   **d)** The company will incur costs

7. **Which of the following are true about product backlog refinement? Select all that apply.**

   **a)** Additional detail is added to the backlog items

   **b)** It's considered an event in Scrum

   **c)** Estimates is added to the backlog items

   **d)** Backlog items can be updated ANYTIME by the Product Owner

8. **Which of the following are true about product backlog refinement? Select all that apply.**

   **a)** It's typically done towards the end of a Sprint

   **b)** The Scrum Team decides when and how it's done

   **c)** This is a continual process

   **d)** The Product Owner and Dev Team collaborate on refinement

9. **Which of the following are true about product backlog refinement? Select all that apply.**

   **a)** It's an activity that's done within the Sprint

   **b)** Its synonymous with backlog grooming

   **c)** Shouldn't consume no more than 10% of Dev Team's capacity

   **d)** Stories should be defined far in advance

10. **Which of the following are true about backlog refinement? Select all that apply.**

   a) While a Product Owner collaborates with the Dev Team, The PO is responsible for final estimates

   b) Higher ordered items on average are clearer than lower ordered ones

   c) Stakeholders should be invited to refinement sessions

   d) Backlog items should be refined enough to complete within a Sprint

11. **What's the main objective of the product backlog refinement session?**

   a) To add items

   b) To remove items

   c) To add additional details to items

   d) To plan future Sprints

12. **What's the maximum amount of time a refinement meeting should take for a one week sprint?**

   a) ½ day

   b) 1 day

   c) 1 ½ days

   d) 2 days

13. **True or False: Backlog refinement should be limited to precisely one occurrence during a 30 day Sprint.**

14. **Select all of the following that are true regarding the Daily Scrum?**

   a) Its 15 minute for a 1-week Sprint, and longer for a 4-week Sprint

   b) It happens every workday of the week during the Sprint

   c) It helps the Scrum Team create a plan for the entire week

   d) It's held at the same place daily

15. **Select all of the following that are true regarding the Daily Scrum?**

   **a)** The entire Scrum Team must attend

   **b)** The Scrum Master is there to orchestrate the event

   **c)** The Scrum Guide recommends each member of the Dev Team to answer 5 questions

   **d)** It helps the Scrum Team synchronize activities

16. **Select all of the following that are true regarding the Daily Scrum?**

   **a)** It's an opportunity for stakeholders to inspect work

   **b)** It's done the same in all companies

   **c)** It's an opportunity to forecast work for the next day

   **d)** Helps the Dev Team apply self-organization

17. **True or False: The Daily Scrum helps the Scrum Team stay on track for the Sprint Goal.**

18. **Select all of the following that are true regarding the Daily Scrum?**

   **a)** The entire team participates

   **b)** It optimizes the chances that the Dev team will obtain the Sprint Goal

   **c)** The Daily Scrum should NEVER exceed 15 minutes

   **d)** None of the above

19. **What's the Scrum Master's role for a Daily Scrum?**

   **a)** To direct each team member to answer the 3 questions

   **b)** To coach the team on the rules for the Daily Scrum

   **c)** To teach The Dev Team to keep it within the 15-minute time box

   **d)** All of the above

20. **Which of the TWO is true about the Daily Scrum?**

   **a)** It's not considered an event in the Sprint

   **b)** Encourages quick decision making

**c)** Eradicates the need for other meetings

**d)** Only rule is that it's time-boxed to 15 minutes

21. **Which of the following TWO is true about the Daily Scrum?**

**a)** It's a time to work on design, testing, and system architecture

**b)** Increases transparency

**c)** Should be facilitated by the same member of The Dev Team

**d)** Increases Dev Teams knowledge about the product

22. **Which of the following can be used for forecasting progress?**

**a)** Burn down charts

**b)** Burn up charts

**c)** Cumulative flows

**d)** Spreadsheets

23. **True or False: The Scrum Master can influence the Product Owner to cancel a Sprint before the time-box elapses.**

24. **True or False: Once a Sprint is initiated its duration cannot be increased or decreased regardless of the circumstance.**

25. **True or False: The Sprint can be classified as a "wrapper" for all of the events in Scrum.**

26. **True or False: Inspection and adaption should ONLY be done during the prescribed events in Scrum?**

27. **True or False: Sprint durations MUST be consistent throughout the duration of the entire project.**

# Chapter IV Answers

1. Choices (a), (b), and (c) are correct. Choice (d) is incorrect because according to The Scrum Guide they restart at the end of the previous Sprint.

2. Choice (b) only. A Sprint can be canceled if the Sprint Goal changes, and while the goal is to create an Increment of DONE product it's not 100% mandatory. Also, the coding is done within the Sprint.

3. Choices (a) and (b) are correct. The Product Owner and Dev Team can negotiate as more is learned, and changes are allowed as long as it doesn't jeopardize the Sprint Goal.

4. Choices (a), (b), and (d) are correct. A Sprint should never exceed a month—if needed, features from the previous Sprint could be rolled over to the next one.

5. Choices (a), (b), and (c) are all correct.

6. Choices (b), (c), and (d) are all correct.

7. Choices (a), (c), and (d) are true. Choice (b) is incorrect because the refinement meeting is not considered an event in Scrum at the time of publication.

8. All of the options are correct. Refer to the section regarding product backlog refinement for additional details.

9. Choices (a), (b), and (c) are correct. Choice (d) is incorrect because defining stories too far in advance means that the requirements could change making the work done on the user-story a waste.

10. Choices (b) and (d) are correct. Choice (a) is incorrect because the Dev Team is responsible for estimates. Choice (c) is incorrect as the Product Owner can instead communicate the desires of the stakeholder to The Dev Team.

11. Choice (c) is the best answer. During the refinement meeting details are added along with estimates and their order in the backlog. Only the items currently in the backlog are tweaked.

12. Choice (a). The Scrum Guide states that refinement meeting shouldn't consume any more than 10% of the development time. Therefore, for an 8-hour day, the allocated time is as follows: for a 1 week Sprint that equates to roughly ½ day, 1 day for two week sprint, 1 ½ days for a 3 week Sprint, and 2 days for a 4 week Sprint.

13. FALSE: It should be held as many times as the team deems fit as long as it doesn't obstruct the team's performance.

14. Choices (b) and (d) are correct. A is incorrect as it's time-boxed to 15 minutes regardless of the duration of the Sprint. Choice (c) is incorrect as the planning is done during the Sprint Planning session.

15. Choice (d) only. The Dev Team is the only member of the team that's required to attend and while The Scrum Master teaches the Dev Team to execute the Daily Scrum their attendance is not needed. Lastly, The Scrum Guide recommends that the Dev Team answer 3 questions not 5 which are: What they did yesterday? What they'll do today? Are there any impediments they're facing?

16. Choices (c) and (d) are correct. Stakeholders should not be present and methodologies for hosting a Daily Scrum may vary from company to company.

17. True. It's a way for them to monitor their progress in obtaining the Sprint Goal.

18. Choices (b) and (c) only. Only The Dev team should participate in the Daily Scrum. If additional time is needed outside the 15 minute time-box then the team should meet immediately to discuss. Refer to the section in Chapter IV about the Daily Scrum for additional details.

19. Choices (b) and (c) are correct. Choice (a) is not correct because they teach The Dev Team the rules of the Daily Scrum but it's up to the Dev Team to direct the flow of the discussion.

20. Choices (b) and (c) only. Choice (a) is incorrect because it is an event in the Sprint, and choice (d) is incorrect because it has more than one rule. I.e. only Dev Team participates, the 3-questions are answered, and it's held at same place daily.

21. Choices (b) and (d) are correct. Choice (a) is incorrect because technical discussions should take place outside the sphere of the Daily Scrum. Choice (c) is incorrect because there's no rule for this in Scrum.

22. All of the above can be used to forecast progress.

23. True. Even though the Product Owner is responsible for canceling the Sprint, they can do so under the influence of any member of the Scrum Team and stakeholders.

24. True. Changing the Sprint duration would prevent the Scrum Team from developing a cadence.

25. Yes. It contains all of the other events in the framework.

26. False. The events are the prescribed times in which inspection and adaption is done. However, there's no rule in Scrum that disallows the team from inspecting and adapting outside the formal events.

27. False. It's recommended but perhaps in the early stages a new Scrum Team need to try different Sprint lengths to see which one is most suitable for them.

# CHAPTER V:

# Closing Phase

The Closing Phase is the activities that concludes the current Sprint and includes the Sprint Review and Retrospective. This is the last portion of the Sprint cycle and is a critical time for the team to generate feedback and make adaptations. Ideally the team has completed the backlog items that they agreed to during the Sprint Planning event so that they can present it to key stakeholders and customers for feedback. After the Sprint Review is completed the Sprint Retrospective follows which is a time for the team to reflect about things that went well, and things that needs improvement. The chapter kicks-off explaining the rules and recommended practices of the Sprint Review so let's get to it.

# Sprint Review

The Sprint Review also known as the "Sprint Demo" is a time-boxed informal meeting that's held at the end of the Sprint, and its main objective is to present the product increment to key stakeholders—this should induce feedback, discussions, and collaborations. This is the event of the Product Owner as they're the one that's responsible for inviting stakeholders, presenting the backlog to them, and explaining what's been done and what hasn't. The Product Owner should try and inspire the stakeholders which will lead them to providing ideas and feedback on the product increment. The event is time-boxed to 4-hours for 1-month Sprints and shorter for Sprints of lesser duration—in order to extract the most value the team should come prepared. There are quite a few misconceptions about the Sprint Review so I created a list of recommended things to do and to avoid.

# The Dos and Don'ts of Sprint Review

**DO LEARN:** This is an excellent time for the Scrum Team and the stakeholders to collectively learn. The team should aim to generate as much feedback as possible from the stakeholders as it's a rare occurrence for everyone to be in the same place discussing the state of the project. The quicker feedback is generated, the quicker the team can formulate a plan of action for optimizing the backlog. It's important that the Scrum Team adapts an open mindset and look forward to receiving the input of the stakeholders. Remember, the developers are not building the software for themselves; they're building it for a targeted audience and should listen to what that audience have to say. Collecting feedback early and often also reduces heartache as the Dev Team will have a clearer understanding of what needs to be done minimizing the probability of doing re-work.

**DO TIME BOX:** Like any other event in Scrum this one is time-boxed to minimize wasted expenditure. The team is allocated a maximum of 4-hours for a one week Sprint, and typically less for Sprints of lesser duration. The Scrum team should collaborate and figure out how to organize the Sprint Review session. If the team is able to get everything done before the time-box expires, then mission accomplished.

**DO PRIORITIZE:** The backlog is not the only thing in Scrum that should be ordered as certain details in the event should be to optimize time. A top-priority with the review is to gain feedback so it should be generated early-on in the event. One way to do this is that instead of the team focusing on acceptance criteria their main priority should be centered on eliciting feedback from the stakeholders. The Dev Team should present the demo early-on which will help get feedback flowing. The quicker the Scrum Team can iterate through a feedback loop the more understanding they'll gain about the software. In order for this to happen the Scrum Team must be proactive in pulling feedback from the stakeholders.

**DO SHOW, TELL, AND COLLABORATE:** One of the objectives of Sprint is to deliver quality, tested, working software—therefore this philosophy should also be adapted during the Sprint Review. Instead of providing stakeholders with screenshots, PowerPoints, printouts, or simulations in an IDE, present them with working software to play with. The Dev Team should explain to what they're looking at along with instructions on how to use it. This is a crucial stage for generating explicit and implicit feedback—while the stakeholders are using the software they'll most likely be discussing things they like along with recommendations for improvement. The Dev Team can also observe the stakeholders' interactions for potential ways to improve certain parameters—for example, if they notice that the stakeholders have a difficult time using the GUI then they might want to think about re-designing it. The demo is not the only object that's revealed to the stakeholders as the backlog and project status should also be made transparent as well. The Scrum Team and stakeholders can collaborate to re-prioritize the backlog to meet any new objectives for the project.

**DO COLLECT VOTES:** Towards the end of the review the Scrum Team can ask the stakeholders to report their satisfaction with the product increment. The team can make this as low-tech or high-tech as they want. They can simply ask the stakeholders to write down their satisfaction from a scale of 1-10 on a sticky note and place it on the board when they leave, or they can use web-survey software to administer it.

**DON'T USE A CUSTOMER PROXY:** The Product Owner should not use a customer proxy during Sprint Review since the stakeholders will be present. They should instead act as a team member and assist with answering any questions that stakeholders may have. The team will gain more value from the meeting if everyone clearly understands their role which is something the Scrum Master coaches the team on.

**DON'T BE BORING:** Similar to the Daily Scrum, there's no reason why the Sprint Review has to be a dull meeting. My recommendation is to make it a celebration especially if the team has worked hard to overcome difficult obstacles. The extent of the party will vary in accordance to the company's culture and philosophy, but this is something that can be discussed while planning the Sprint Review. I'm not advocating a lavish expensive wine party, but more so an economical and DIY type of theme party. Also, a couple of pizzas wouldn't be a bad idea because conversation can flow nicely with a delicious slice of pizza.

**DON'T COME UNPREPARED:** The Scrum Team should collaborate beforehand to structure the meeting. A clear agenda should be made along with checkpoints for topics of interest. The team should also script the process so that everyone will know when it's their turn to talk and what to say—this should be done until the team is confident that they can seamlessly run the event. The team should ensure that the demo is tested thoroughly and that it'll be ready to be used upon the arrival of the stakeholders.

**DON'T GET TOO TECHNICAL:** The stakeholders more than likely won't understand the technical details within this timeframe and nor do they need to. Instead, they want to see if the increment produces business value which is why I recommend that they should be given time to experiment with the demo hands-on.

# The Group Roles during Review

To gain a better understanding of the Sprint Review I'm going to list the invitees with descriptions of their roles. The entire Scrum Team attends the review along with the key stakeholders who the Product Owner invites. This is the only prescribed event in the framework in which the Scrum Team and the stakeholders are required to collaborate.

## THE SCRUM MASTER

The Scrum Master makes sure that the event occurs and that everyone understands its rules and purpose. Since the Scrum Master is the guardian of Scum knowledge they educate everyone on the rules of the meeting such as keeping it within the allocated time-box. They also ensure that everyone is clear about the purpose of the event which is for both parties to collaborate in order to generate feedback.

## THE PRODUCT OWNER

They're the main contributor on the Scrum Team during the Sprint Review. They elaborate on what stories meet the criteria of done and which stories do not. This is the time in which transparency is important. If there are incomplete stories then the Product Owner should inform the stakeholders along with plans that the team has created to resolve it in order to gain their confidence. The Product Owner should reveal the current state of the backlog along with the outstanding work remaining for the project. The common method of choice is burn down charts, and they can compare the burn down chart of the current Sprint to those of the previous ones.

## THE DEV TEAM ROLE

They showcase the working demo to the attendees and are prepared to answer any questions they may have. It's important that the Dev Team don't elaborate in too much technical detail as this can sway away from the agenda of the meeting. In addition, they may list what went well during the tenure of the Sprint, what impediments they faced, and the solutions they used to resolve it.

## THE GROUP'S ROLE

Both the Scrum Team and the stakeholders must work together to determine what's the next step for the project. The input into the Sprint Review is the product increment while the output is an optimized product backlog that forecasts the backlog items for the upcoming Sprint.

# Sprint Retrospective

This is the final event in Scrum and occurs between the Sprint Review and the next Sprint Planning meeting. Its main purpose is for the Scrum Team to reflect upon the occurrences in the previous Sprint and to decide what needs to change and what needs to remain the same. Even though the Daily Scrum is a key event for inspecting and adapting, the Sprint Retrospective is allocated more time and is dedicated solely to improving the team's workflow. For a 1-month Sprint the time-box for this event is reserved to 3-hours, and typically less for Sprints of shorter duration.

Like all of the events in Scrum, the Scrum Master is the team member that's responsible for educating the team about the rules and its purpose. According to the Scrum Guide there are three main purposes of the retrospective: One, Inspect the last Sprint by analyzing the people, relationships, processes and tools used, two, discover what the team did well and what needs improvement and three, devise a plan for integrating the improvements within the Scrum Team. For the first point I would recommend categorizing the section of each item and then soliciting the team's feedback. The team can have a couple of minutes to themselves to reflect upon the past Sprint and think about things that they can personally improve upon. In terms of relationships the team can suggest ways on how they can develop and maintain better work relationships amongst each other. When it comes to processes and tools each developer can write down their thoughts if something needs to change or if it remains the same. If a change is needed then the developer should be succinct on their suggestion. The sticky note can then be placed on the whiteboard and then read out loud to the entire team. The team could use a consensus voting method such as the fist-of-five or Dotmocracy to determine if a change is needed. Once the team has agreed on a consensus on what needs to change they need to collaboratively prioritize this data.

My advice is for the team to prioritize the backlog by predicting the benefit that changing that variable will have.

For example, if the team is using project management software that has been presenting issues to the team then they could consider switching to another type of software. They will need to weigh the tradeoffs of this decision such as additional costs and consumed resources since the team will go through a learning phase. Once the team has prioritized their items they will then build a plan that's feasible for them to execute. The items for improvement can be revisited often in the subsequent Daily Scrums. The next section will go over some recommended practices for conducting your retrospective.

# BEST PRACTICES

**DON'T BE REPETITIVE:** There are many ways to add variety to retrospectives so don't redundantly do the same thing each Sprint. The team can experiment with different methods for getting to the root cause of issues other than sticky notes. Some of the methods that they could consider trying are the 5 Whys or the Socratic Method. Other variables that the team could consider testing are the location that the event takes place. The team could consider discussing some of the details of the retrospective over lunch and then filling in the specifics once they get back to office. There are many possibilities so the team should in effect do a retrospective within a retrospective and figure out ways to make the event more engaging.

**LIMIT ITEMS ON THE WISH LIST:** There are only so many hours in a day and it's unreasonable for the Scrum Team to try and improve on 50 total items within a Sprint! This is why prioritizing the list of items is critical, so that the team doesn't get stuck with too much overhead—it's ironic but possible that the team can become less productive by trying to make too many changes in a short duration.

To limit the number of items that make it to the improvement list, each developer should have a ceiling for the number of suggestions they can make. It's also important for the team to collectively rate the difficulty of the change to implement so that they can gauge if it's a realistic implementation for them.

**FOCUS ON THINGS THE TEAM CAN CONTROL:** There are some variables that the team has control over, and there are other things that they don't. Things like what their competitors are doing, what decisions upper-management are making, and the eccentric clothing that the CEO wears are unfortunately some of the things they can't control. However, the way that they get work done is within their locus on control so there's no point to harp-on outside factors. The team should have tunnel-vision and be determined to discover ways to improve upon the factors they can control. Leave the complaints at home, even if the company CEO routinely wears a sports blazer paired with tropical shorts and Cowboy Boots. One topic that I like to bring up is how the team can double, triple, or even quadruple their velocity? It's probably a far stretch, but it's an interesting question to mention during this event.

**TALK ABOUT THE GOOD AND THE BAD:** The team needs to exude transparency to one another for effective reflecting. It's never a bad idea for a team member to mention when one of their colleagues have contributed something monumental to the project. It's natural for employees to like being recognized in front of their peers. However, the team needs to be able to manage constructive criticism. I'm not an advocate of public bashing as that'll more than likely lead to poor employee morale which wont contribute to team building. However, if something is negatively affecting the state of the project then it needs to be done so in a professional manner. The team can't improve if they only acknowledge their strengths and fail to look at their weaknesses.

**LIMIT STAKEHOLDERS AND MANAGERS:** This event is reserved for the Scrum Team only. There should be a big sign outside the entrance that says "No Stakeholders allowed!" Well, that's taken things a little too far but in all seriousness the retrospective should be an event in which the Scrum Team can communicate openly and honestly with one another. A stakeholder's presence may prevent that from happening. They get to stay informed of the project status each Sprint during the Sprint Review or when needed by getting in contact with the Product Owner. However, the retrospective is not a time for strict-management as it's reserved solely for the team to reflect upon the previous Sprint.

# Chapter V Rewind

This chapter put the finishing touches on the Scrum Framework and discussed the components that take place after the duration of the Sprint which are the Sprint Review and the Sprint Retrospective. The Sprint Review is an event in which the Scrum Team presents a demo of the product increment to the key stakeholders. The presentation should invoke conversation and feedback from the stakeholders which will help both parties have a better understanding of the future product. The Sprint Retrospective is the final event of Scrum and is a time for reflection for the team. They analyze what went well, what needs improvement, and devise a plan on how to implement changes within the next Sprint.

# Chapter V Resources

Schwaber, Ken, and Jeff Sutherland. The Scrum Guide. July/August 2016. Accessed August 1, 2016. http://www.scrumguides.org/docs/scrumguide/v2016/2016-Scrum-Guide-US.pdf.

# Chapter V Quiz

1. **Which of the following TWO is true about the Sprint Review?**

   a) It CAN be held mid-Sprint if stakeholders request it

   b) The workflow of the Dev Team is inspected

   c) It's held at towards the end of the Sprint

   d) It's a prime opportunity for teammates to rate each other

2. **Which of the following TWO is true about the Sprint Review?**

   a) The entire Scrum Team and stakeholders collaborate

   b) Scrum suggests that the Dev Team answer 4 questions

   c) The Product Backlog is modified if needed

   d) Scrum suggests that a PowerPoint presentation is used

3. **Which of the following TWO statements is true about the Sprint Review?**

   a) It's considered a formal meeting

   b) It's considered an informal meeting

   c) The Sprint Backlog should be updated

   d) Feedback is encouraged

4. **Which of the following TWO is true about the Sprint Review?**

   a) The Scrum Master is responsible for ensuring that it happens

   b) It's time boxed to 4-hours for all Sprints

   c) Everyone on the Scrum Team should participate

   d) It's a status meeting

**5.** **Which of the following TWO is true about the Sprint Review?**

    **a)** Stakeholders and the Product Owner only collaborates

    **b)** Stakeholders and the Scrum Team collaborates on what was done for the Sprint

    **c)** Stakeholders and Scrum Team collaborate on what to do next

    **d)** Stakeholders and Dev Team only collaborates while Scrum Master time-box the event

**6.** **Which of the following TWO is true about the Sprint Review?**

    **a)** The Scrum Master invites key stakeholders

    **b)** The Scrum Master ensures that everyone understands its purpose

    **c)** The Product Owner explains which backlog items are complete and incomplete

    **d)** The full product is expected to be done

**7.** **Which of the following TWO is true about the Sprint Review?**

    **a)** The Dev Team could state what went well and what obstacles they're facing

    **b)** The Dev Team makes forecasts for the completion date of project

    **c)** The Dev Team shows the work they completed

    **d)** The Dev Team request changes to the stakeholders

**8.** **Which of the following TWO is true about the Sprint Review?**

    **a)** The Product Owner forecasts completion dates for the project

    **b)** The Increment is given a numerical score by the stakeholders

    **c)** The marketplace is analyzed

    **d)** The plan for the next Sprint is finalized

**9.** **Which of the following TWO is true about the Sprint Review?**

    **a)** The most valuable thing to do next is discussed

    **b)** Ineffective members of the Scrum Team are released

**c)** The budget is reviewed

**d)** None of the above

10. **True or False: The timeline, budget, and marketplace are reviewed before the next pending release of the product.**

11. **True or False: The output of the Sprint Review is a modified Product Backlog that shows potential backlog items for the next month**

12. **Select all of the following that are true about Sprint Retrospectives?**

    **a)** It occurs after the Sprint Review

    **b)** Only the Product Owner and the Dev Team participate

    **c)** It's time-boxed to three hours for all Sprints

    **d)** It's an excellent opportunity for the team to inspect itself

13. **Select all of the following that are true about Sprint Retrospectives?**

    **a)** A 1 month Sprint will typically have a time-box of less than three hours

    **b)** The Product Owner makes sure that the event takes place

    **c)** The Sprint Retrospective is outside the Sprint

    **d)** The Scrum Master makes sure the Scrum Team understands its purpose

14. **Select all of the following that are true about the Sprint Retrospectives?**

    **a)** It analyzes how people, relationships and processes are developing

    **b)** It's typically not time-boxed

    **c)** There are no outputs

    **d)** The Scrum Master participates as a peer team member

15. **Select all of the following that are true about Sprint Retrospectives?**

    **a)** The Scrum Team identifies improvements for the next Sprint

    **b)** The Scrum Master ensures everyone understands its purpose

    **c)** The team discusses what went well and what didn't

    **d)** The team devises a plan for improving the process

## 16. Which team member is responsible for releasing the product increment?

    **a)** Scrum Master

    **b)** Product Owner

    **c)** Dev Team

    **d)** Stakeholder

# Chapter V Quiz Answers

1. Choices (c) only. Choice (a) is incorrect because it doesn't make sense to have a Sprint Review mid-Sprint if the Increment is not complete. Choice (b) is incorrect as the Increment is inspected during this event, not the workflow of the developers. Choice (d) is incorrect because the Sprint Review is not the right opportunity to do this.

2. Choices (a) and (c) are correct. Scrum doesn't explicitly propose any questions during the Sprint Review, and it doesn't suggest any presentation format for the Increment.

3. Choices (b) and (d) are correct. The Sprint Review is considered an informal meeting so choice (a) is incorrect. Also, choice (c) is incorrect because the backlog should be updated not the Sprint Backlog.

4. Choices (a) and (c) are correct. The Daily Scrum is time-boxed to 4 hours only for 4-week Sprints, but it's typically shorter for Sprints of shorter duration. Also, it's not classified as a status meeting since it's considered informal.

5. Choices (b) and (c) are true. The entire Scrum Team and stakeholders collaborate making options (a) and (d) incorrect.

6. Choices (b) and (c) are correct. The Product Owner invites the stakeholders, and the Increment of the recent Sprint only is expected to be done otherwise noted.

7. Choices (a) and (c) are correct. The Product Owner is the member that will make projections if needed which makes (b) invalid. Also,

the stakeholders will more than likely be the ones making change requests, and The Dev team can provide their feedback on those requests which makes (d) invalid.

8.  Choices (a) and (c) are correct. Choice (b) is incorrect because while the stakeholders can discuss the details of the Increment, they're not required to give it a numerical score. Choice (d) is incorrect because while backlog items for the next Sprint may be discussed, it's not actually finalized until the end of the next Sprint Planning session

9.  Choices (a) and (c) are correct. Choice (c) is not something that will be discussed during the Sprint Review.

10. True. Refer to the Sprint Review section in Chapter V for additional details.

11. True. The Sprint Review session will illicit feedback from stakeholders which will most likely lead to an updated backlog.

12. Choices (a) and (d) are correct. Choice (b) is incorrect because the entire Scrum Team should participate and (c) is incorrect because the Sprint Retrospective is time-boxed to three hours for a 1-month Sprint.

13. Choices (a) and (d) are true. Choice (b) is incorrect as that's the Scrum Master Job, and (c) is incorrect because it's considered part of the Sprint.

14. Choices (a) and (d) are correct. Since the Sprint Retrospective is an event it's time-boxed to three hours max for a one month Sprint. Choice (c) is incorrect as there are outputs such as a plan for implementing the improvements the team has identified.

15. All of these options are correct. Refer to the section in Chapter V about Sprint Retrospectives.

16. Choice (b) is correct. The Product Owner is the owner of the product backlog is responsible for managing the releases.

# The Awesome
# Agile Resource

The following list contains information concerning certifications related to various project management and process improvement methods. This resource may be of use to those who are interested in advancing or changing careers. I would like to warn those seeking certifications of a couple of points. They may help get you into the door for an interview but it's what you say afterwards that'll increase your chances of landing the job. Also, I'll recommend using this resource as a starting point to carry out additional research. When selecting an organization for certification I would recommend three tips: analyze the organization's credibility, the quality of their teaching material, and how in-demand it is. The web changes at a brisk pace and all URLs, certification costs, and test format information was accurate at the time of publication. If any of the information is outdated by the time you read it then send me a query here: doug@purcellconsult.com.

# ScrumandAgileCertifications

## SCRUM ORG

https://www.scrum.org

This organization was founded by Ken Schwaber in 2009 and is dedicated to teaching software practitioners how to soundly apply Scrum principles to the workplace. The website provides an array of resources such as: open assessments, courses, certifications, community, and resources. They offer several 2-day public courses for the various certifications that they offer. The prices for the public courses range from roughly $995 to $1995. Individuals who complete a public course will also have the opportunity to get certified at no additional cost. They offer several types of certifications such as Professional Scrum Master (PSM I, II, & III), Professional Scrum Product Owner (PSPO I & II), Professional Scrum Developer (PSD I), and Scaled Professional Scrum (SPS).

### PSM I certification
The cost to get your PSM I certification is $150 per assessment at the time of publication. The PSM I test format is multiple choice, multiple answer, and True/False. You get 60 minutes to complete 80 questions or 45 seconds per question, and you must score at least an 85% or answer a minimum of 68 questions correctly.

### PSM II certification
To get PSM II certified it costs $500, but if you take the PSM I first then you get a $200 discount. The PSM II test format is multiple choice, case-study, and essay. Test-takers get 90 minutes to complete the test and must score at least an 85% to get certified.

### PSM III certification
The PSM III assessment is available to those who have successfully cleared the PSM I and II assessments. It's the most difficult certification for Scrum Masters and those who take it should have a comprehensive knowledge of the framework along with the skills to teach and coach teams. The test is in multiple choice/essay format, and test-takers get 120 minutes to complete the assessment. A minimum score of 85% is required to past. The assessment costs $500 to take.

### PSPO I certification
To get PSPO I certified costs $200—the test format is multiple choice, multiple answer, and true/false. You get 60 minutes to answer 80 questions.

### PSPO II certification
The PSPO II costs $500 per assessment and you get a $200 discount if you took a PSPO course first. The test format consists of multiple choice, case study questions, and essays.

### PSD I
At the time of publication there's only one certification for developers which is the PSD I. It costs $200 to complete the assessment and is in multiple choice/ true or false format. The test has a total of 80 questions and a time-cap of 60 minutes. Like the previous certifications you need to score a minimum of 85% to pass.

### Scaled Professional Scrum (SPS)
This is a certification that's based on the Nexus Framework, which is a process for scaling Scrum across multiple teams. Each assessment costs $250, and the test format is multiple choice, multiple answer, and true/false. You get 60 minutes to answer 40 questions, or 1.5 minutes per question. You need to score at least an 85 or answer 34 questions correctly.

Compared to Scrum Alliance you don't need to take a public or private course in order to get certified from Scrum.org, but obviously it's recommended to do diligent studying. Reading this book, completing the exercises, and taking the open assessments at Scrum.org should help you prepare diligently for the PSM and PSPO certifications. Those who get certified will have their name appear on the online database of certified Scrum Professionals.

## RELATED LINKS

- Homepage: `https://www.scrum.org`
- Open Assessments: `https://www.scrum.org/Assessments/Open-Assessments`
- Facebook: `https://www.facebook.com/Scrum.org`
- LinkedIn: `https://www.linkedin.com/company/scrum-org`
- Scrum community: `https://www.scrum.org/Community`

# SCRUM ALLIANCE

This nonprofit organization is the largest Agile certifying body and membership in the world with 450,000 certified practitioners globally. In addition to offering certification they also host Scrum events and discussions. They offer four types of certifications which are for practitioners, trainers, coaches, and registered education providers (REPs). All certifications come with access to two years to the Scrum Alliance. Below is a breakdown of the current certifications for aspiring or current Scrum practitioners.

## CERTIFIED SCRUM MASTER® (CSM)

There are two steps to completing your CSM certificate. One, you must attend a 16-hour CSM course from a Scrum Alliance Authorized Trainer. Two, you'll need to pass the CSM test with a score of at least 24 out of 35 or roughly 69%. The average costs for the course ranges from roughly $ $800 to $1295 USD.

## CERTIFIED SCRUM PRODUCT OWNER (CSPO)

There's just one step to getting certified which is to attend a two-day CSPO course taught by a Certified Scrum Trainer. The average costs for the course ranges from roughly $999 to $1395 USD.

## CERTIFIED SCRUM DEVELOPER (CSD)

Becoming CSD is the most demanding of the certifications offered by Scrum Alliance. In order to become certified you must complete at least five days of training taught by a Scrum Alliance Registered Education Provider (REP), and a Scrum Alliance Authorized Instructor. The certification is valid for two years, and there are two recommended tracks. One, you can take a CSM course for two days, and a CSD *Agile Engineering Practices* course for 3 days. Two, you can take a 1-day CSD intro course, 3-day CSD *Agile Engineering Practices* technical course, and 1-day CSD Technical Elective course. You can take a course that completes all requirements for the CSD for around $3250 regular or $2750 if you register early.

## CERTIFIED SCRUM PROFESSIONAL (CSP)

There are three criteria that one must meet in order to become CSP certified. One, they must have a CSM, CSPO, or CSD certification. Two, they must have at least 36-month's worth of experience in a Scrum role, and lastly they must submit 70 Scrum Education Units (SEUs) form the past three years. The total costs for the certification is $250.

## RELATED LINKS

- Scrum User Groups: `https://www.scrumalliance.org/community/user-groups`
- Worldwide Scrum Gatherings: `https://www.scrumalliance.org/courses-events/events/global-gatherings`
- Scrum Learning Resources: `https://www.scrumalliance.org/why-scrum/scrum-resources`
- How to become a certified Scrum trainer without taking the two day course?

# AGILE CERTIFIED PRACTITIONER PMI-ACP

`http://www.pmi.org/certifications/types/agile-acp`

The Project Management Institute (PMI) is a US based non-profit organization founded in 1969 that's dedicated to project management. In the 1970s standardization accounted for less than 20% of the institute efforts, but by the 1980s a bigger effort was made to promote standardization within project management processes. This is a large institution, with current members exceeding 450,000 in more than 200 countries. The PMI has several types of certifications but only one relevant to Agile which is the PMI Agile Certified Practitioner (PMI-ACP). This test covers several Agile-related topics such as: Scrum, Kanban, Lean, Test-Driven Development (TDD), and Extreme Programming (XP). The test costs $435 for PMI members or $495 for nonmembers—it costs $129 to join the PMI with a $129 renewal fee. There's also a $10 application fee for new members. If you fail the test first time around no need to hyperventilate as you'll get two more chances to retake it within a year. However, the economical route would be to pass it the first time around so you won't have to pay the re-take fees.

The format of the PMI-ACP is as follow. It's a 120 question, multiple-choice, 3-hour test with only 100 questions being counted. PMI uses a company called Prometric to administer tests, and they use a technique called "psychometric analysis" to generate the scores. This is a specialized method that analyzes psychological tests and measurements to verify that exams meet industry standards. The drawback to this is that the PMI doesn't explicitly define a passing score. However, it has been the general consensus online that a score of roughly 70% would get you certified. Of course aiming for a higher score doesn't hurt. There are some restrictions that a test-taker must meet before they can take the test. The requirements are a secondary degree, 12 months experience working on project teams, 1500 hours working on teams applying Agile methodologies, and 21 training hours in Agile practices. In addition, you must get 30 professional development units (PDUs) within a 3-year cycle in order to maintain your certification. There are a variety of ways in which you can earn your PDUs. You can do this by taking any of the PMI® published quizzes, volunteering at local chapters, and publishing content related to project management.

## RELATED LINKS

- PMI-ACP ® Handbook: `http://www.pmi.org/Certification/~/media/PDF/Certifications/PMI-ACP_Handbook.ashx`
- PMI-ACP Examination Content Outline: `http://www.pmi.org/en/Certification/~/media/Files/PDF/Agile/PMI_Agile_Certification_Content_Outline.ashx`
- Facebook: `https://www.facebook.com/PMInstitute`
- Twitter: `https://twitter.com/PMInstitute`
- Linkedin: `https://www.linkedin.com/company/project-management-institute`
- Google+: `https://plus.google.com/u/0/+pmi/posts`
- YouTube: `https://www.youtube.com/user/PMInstitute`

# LARGE SCALE SCRUM (LeSS)

`https://less.works`

Large Scale Scrum (LeSS) is a framework for scaling Agile across large teams. It has been implemented on teams ranging from 2-2500 people. To get certified in Large Scale Scrum (LeSS) you must take a certified Large Scale Scrum (LeSS) Practitioner course which is 3-days that varies by price per instructor, but is usually around $2550.

Once you complete the course you'll automatically become a certified practitioner and will get an account made for you on *less.works*. The certifications are good for two years and after that time has elapsed you'll need to pay a renewal fee in order to retain it.

# Scaled Agile Framework (SAFe)

http://www.scaledagile.com

This is the official certifying organization for the Scaled Agile Framework (SAFe). This was founded by Dean Leffingwell, Colin O'Neil and, Drew Jemilo back in 2011 to humble beginnings but now have a corporate headquarters in Boulder Colorado. They offer several types of certifications with one of the most popular ones being the SAFe Agilist (SA) which introduces the SAFe framework. In order to get certified you must take a class which prepares you for the exam, and then pass it with a score of at least 50%. You must renew your certification yearly at the cost of $100 and get at least 10 continuing education hours. The price of the 2-day course will vary by instructor.

# Project Management Certifications

## PMP

https://www.pmi.org/certifications/types/project-management-pmp

The PMI's very first certification credential was the Project Management Professional (PMP®) which was started in 1984. It along with Prince2 has become one of the most desirable project management certifications internationally. At the time of publication there were over 700,000 individuals with a PMP and 27 chartered chapters in other 200+ territorial globally. PMP is a unique certification as it's an agnostic project management strategy that can be applied to a wide array of industries. There are two ways to meet the prerequisites to take the PMO. One, you must have a secondary degree of equivalent, 7,500 hours leading projects, and 35-hours of project management certification. Two, you must have a four-year degree, 4,500 hours leading projects, and 35 hours of project management education. The cost to take the PMP is $405 for PMI members and $555 for non-members. The test is 200-questions and in multiple choice format. The test focuses on the five major components of process groups which are initiating, planning, executing, monitoring/controlling, and closing. Test-takers have an opportunity to re-take the test two times within a year, paying a retake fee each time.

### RELATED LINKS

- PMBOK ® Guide and Standards: http://www.pmi.org/pmbok-guide-standards
- Certifications: http://www.pmi.org/certifications
- PMI Membership: http://www.pmi.org/membership
- Events: http://www.pmi.org/events
- Store: http://www.pmi.org/pmbok-guide-standards

# PRINCE2

`https://www.prince2.com`

This is a global accreditation organization for project management professionals with offices globally. They offer two types of certifications which are PRINCE2 Foundation and PRINCE2 Practitioner. The Prince2 Foundation Exam is a 75-question multiple choice test that you get 60 minutes to complete. Five of the questions won't count towards your final score, so you need to get at least 35 out of 70 questions correct or 50% to pass the test. The test costs $520 to take. You can't take the Practitioner or less you have passed the Foundation Exam or an equivalent replacement such as a PMP or IPMA Level A-D certification. Like the Foundation Exam it costs $520 to take the test and your fee will gain you access to a web-portal for 12-months that contains exercises and a process walkthrough to help reinforce concepts. If you plan on taking the Prince2 Foundation and Practitioner test, then you can get a 12.5% discount and save $130 by ordering them together.

## RELATED LINKS

- Prince 2 Downloads & Resources: `https://www.prince2.com/uk/downloads`
- Facebook: `https://www.facebook.com/Prince2Blog`
- Twiiter: `https://twitter.com/prince2blog`

# BLOGS/WEBSITES

## XEBIA

`http://blog.xebia.com`

This blog features a multitude of Agile practitioners that discuss a variety of topics. You can find articles related to Agile estimates, testing, communication, and anything far in between. This is not a step-by-step primer but a way for experienced practitioners to discover new insights.

# VERSION ONE

http://www.versionone.com/resources/blogs

This is an award winning software development company that has been creating Agile management software since 2002. They're passionate about Agile and have sponsored over 100 events since its inception. In addition to rolling out quality software they also host an informative blog. It's broken up into three sections which are: product blog, Agile management software, and developer's blog.

## Scaled Agile Framework (SAFe) Blog

http://www.scaledagileframework.com/blog

This is the official blog for the Scaled Agile Framework and contains mostly posts by Dean Leffingwell. The blog contains SAFe news, case studies, and an array of topics that pertain to the framework.

## CollabNet

http://blogs.collab.net/agile#.VzaGHZErLNN

This is a software development company that was founded by Tim O'Reilly and Brian Behlendorf in August 1999. The company created several popular products such as Subversion, CloudForge, and TeamForge. In addition to their software products they offer several services and solutions such as consulting, training, implementation, and hosted services. They have a company blog that's frequently updated by employees and contains posts regarding industry news, emerging trends, and company updates. Some of the popular tags on their site related to Agile are listed below:

- Scrum: http://blogs.collab.net/tag/scrum
- Agile development: http://blogs.collab.net/tag/agile-development
- Continuous integration: http://blogs.collab.net/tag/continuous-integration

# MOUNTAIN GOAT SOFTWARE

https://www.mountaingoatsoftware.com/blog

This is a popular blog owned and published by Mike Cohn. He's a prolific writer as he has published three books related to Agile, and he keeps his blog updated by posting several times a month.

# ROMAN PICHLER

http://www.romanpichler.com/blog

This blog is created by author, consultant, Product Owner, and Scrum trainer Roman Pichler. He also makes an extensive amount of posts about product strategy/roadmaps, user-stories, and backlogs.

# MARTIN FOWLER

http://martinfowler.com

This blog is published by Martin Fowler who's a British software developer, public speaker, and prolific author. He published several books on software development and methodologies. Some of the topics he published about are: refactoring, enterprise application architecture, UML, NoSQL, Domain Specific Language (DSL), and Extreme Programming. He has had several books translated into several different languages and was one of the 17 co-authors of the Agile Manifesto. His blog contains a large amount of posts since he's been publishing since 2000. I would recommend reading his getting started guide if you're new to his site: **http://martinfowler.com/intro.html.** There's also a six part interview with Martin Fowler that was conducted by Bill Venners back in 2002: *http://www.artima.com/intv/martin.html.* The topics covered includes: Refactoring, Design Principles, Evolutionary Design, Flexibility, Test-Driven Development, and Performance, and is very insightful.

# AGILE SCOUT

http://agilescout.com

This site was created by Peter Saddington who's a software developer, certified Scrum Master, and published author. His blog posts features listicles and humorous posts related to Scrum.

# CRISP BLOG

http://blog.crisp.se

This blog belongs to an Agile consultancy based in Stockholm Sweden. It features posts from a multitude of developers and Agile coaches about topics of interests. Their blog contains many slides from keynote presentations from their bloggers which will further your knowledge about Agile methodologies.

# ELEGANT CODE

http://elegantcode.com

This is a blogging community that features an array of software developers. Some of the topics include Agile, Scrum, and software development.

# ALL ABOUT AGILE

http://www.allaboutagile.com

This is blog features various bloggers with experience in the software industry. This is a sister site of *101 Ways* which is an Agile consultancy.

# PERSONAL KANBAN

http://www.personalkanban.com/pk/blog

This blog is maintained by author and consultant Jim Benson, and its primary focus is Kanban. There are interviews of software developers discussing their use of Kanban along with video posts revealing concepts based on Kanban.

# KEN SCHWABER BLOG

https://kenschwaber.wordpress.com

This blog is hosted by Ken Schwaber one of the co-founders of Scrum. The blog contains many posts about his opinions, theories, and thought provoking questions related to software development. Even though he doesn't post to it frequently, there's a wealth of information that one can prune to complement their learning of Scrum.

# JEFF SUTHERLAND BLOG

https://www.scruminc.com/scrum-blog

This is a blog by the other co-founder of Scrum Jeff Sutherland and it contains posts of book reviews, software development insights, and news related to his company.

# JASON YIP

http://jchyip.blogspot.de

This blog is written by Agile coach Jason Yip and has tips on how to learn Agile, potential solutions to common agile problems, and tips on how he likes to approach Agile based upon his experience.

# EXTREME PROGRAMMING ORG

http://www.extremeprogramming.org

This was one of the first sites to publish information about Extreme Programming. It was created in 1999 by Don Wells and contains articles, anecdotes, and charts related to XP.

# AGILE MEDIA SITES AND AGGREGATORS

## INFO WORLD

`http://www.infoworld.com/category/agile-development`

This information technology media company was founded back in 1978 by educator Jim Warren who sold it to IDG in 1979—IDG is the company that publishes the "For Dummies" self-help series. It was originally a monthly printed magazine but due to changes in the market it switched to a web-based magazine solely in 2007. Info World is located in the hub of technological advancement, San Francisco and publishes emerging trends in the technology sector. They have a team of seasoned technologists and journalists that post about open source, application development, cloud computing, databases, data center, operation systems security, and storage.

## ALLTOP

Agile: `http://agile.alltop.com`

This site was founded by venture capitalist, author, and former Apple employee Guy Kawasaki. The site aggregates content from top news sites and blogs. They have a section that's dedicated to Agile, project management, and leadership. This is convenient for those who would rather use an aggregator to stay informed about industry news.

- Project management: `http://project-management.alltop.com`
- Leadership: `http://leadership.alltop.co`m

## REDDIT

`https://www.reddit.com/r/scrum`

This popular social news site was started by University of Virginia roommates Steve Huffmann and Alexis Ohanian back in 2005. The site hosts numerous categories that are known as a "subreddit." There's a subreddit for just about every topic you can imagine. Reddit can provide unbiased and occasionally crude discussions regarding topics of interests.

- Agile Development Reddit: `https://www.reddit.com/r/agile`
- Project management: `https://www.reddit.com/r/projectmanagement`

# Digital Bonuses

As advertised, there are three digital bonuses that the reader can take advantage of to assist them with their implementation of Scrum. The instructions of how to utilize each of the bonuses are accompanied by each description.

## PRODUCT BACKLOG (GOOGLE SHEETS)

Here is a product backlog template: **https://goo.gl/gyBKk6**

You can download the file and convert it to one of several extensions such as: xlsx, osd, pdf, html, zipped, csv, or tsv format. To do so click file on the upper-left hand corner of the screen and then select "Download as."

## BURN DOWN CHART TEMPLATE (GOOGLE SHEETS)

The burn down chart template which was used as an example in this book is available. You are free to modify, extend, etc. You can download it via Google Sheets here: **https://goo.gl/cJyWMw**

You can download the file and convert it to one of several extensions such as: xlsx, osd, pdf, html, zipped, csv, or tsv format. To do so click file on the upper-left hand corner of the screen and then select "Download as."

## STORY CARD TEMPLATE (GOOGLE DOCS)

A blank user-story template is provided that's 3 x 5 inches so that you can printout and write on.

You can download it here: **https://goo.gl/2UoJNJ**

You can download and print the file for use at your convenience.

# Index

www.ingramcontent.com/pod-product-compliance
Lightning Source LLC
Chambersburg PA
CBHW052141070326
40690CB00047B/1336